WEIRD-O-PEDIA

WEIRD-O-PEDIA

The Ultimate Book of Surprising, Strange, and
Incredibly Bizarre Facts About (Supposedly) Ordinary Things

ALEX PALMER

Skyhorse Publishing

Skyhorse Publishing books may be purchased in bulk at special discounts for sales promotion, corporate gifts, fund-raising, or educational purposes. Special editions can also be created to specifications. For details, contact the Special Sales Department, Skyhorse Publishing, 307 West 36th Street, 11th Floor, New York, NY 10018 or info@skyhorsepublishing.com.

Skyhorse® and Skyhorse Publishing® are registered trademarks of Skyhorse Publishing, Inc.®, a Delaware corporation.

Visit our website at www.skyhorsepublishing.com.

10 9 8 7 6 5 4 3 2 1

Library of Congress Cataloging-in-Publication Data available on file.

ISBN: 978-1-61608-648-0

Printed in China

WEIRD-O-PEDIA

contents

INTRODUCTION

Wherever you happen to be right now, as you read this sentence, stop for a moment and look around.

You may be lying in a park enjoying a nice sunny day, or on a crowded bus trying to block out a person next to you talking on his cell phone. You may be standing by a shelf in a bookstore, deciding whether the book in your hand is worth taking all the way to the cashier and purchasing. But whatever you are doing, look around.

See something weird?

Of course you do.

It might not be "weird" like a two-headed Gila monster shuffling by in a tiny top hat, or a woman dressed as a giant raspberry doing backflips. It might just be a coffee mug, or an easy chair, or a dandelion. It could be something you've seen every day for years, and never thought of as anything but unremarkable.

But it's weird.

We are surrounded by the bizarre, and the most mundane things in our lives are packed with surprises. This book tries to peel the "normal" away from so many everyday things, from the food we eat to the stuff we keep in our medicine cabinets, to reveal the strangeness underneath.

That dust in your living room is actually making the air cleaner (see "Dust," Chapter 8). The beer you had with dinner is a great way to help your body recover from a run (see "Running," Chapter 7). The cell phone that guy on the bus is using contains about 18 times more dangerous germs than the flush handle in a public restroom (see "Mobile Phones," Chapter 9).

Below are hundreds of odd tidbits about the world around us, and the strange goings on happening inside our own minds and bodies. These facts may crack you up, get you thinking, or keep you up at night worrying about brain-eating amoebae (see "Swimming," Chapter 7) or that in a matter of years bananas may cease to exist (see "Bananas," Chapter 1).

If you have any doubt about the accuracy of these curiosities, or want to read more, flip to the "Sources" section at the back of the book. You will find that as strange as they may sound, or as much as you would like to believe they could not possibly be true, these facts are as genuine as the book in your hand.

Or the shoes on your feet.

Or the zombie orb spider in your backyard, mindlessly following orders from the parasitic wasp babies growing inside of it (see "Wasps," Chapter 10).

CHAPTER 1

FOOD & DRINK

Weird facts about what you put in your body

APPLE PIE

Apple pie is not actually American. English apple pie recipes go back to the time of Chaucer, though these "apple pies" were baked in straight-sided, free-standing crusts, usually without sugar—quite a bit different from the pies that Americans celebrate today.

The first cookbook written and published in America, Amelia Simmons' *American Cookery, or the art of dressing viands, fish, poultry, and vegetables, and the best modes of making pastes, puffs, pies, tarts, puddings, custards, and preserves, and all kinds of cakes, from the imperial plum to plain cake: Adapted to this country, and all grades of life,* from 1796, includes four recipes for apple pastries. That's the same number given to all the other fruit pastries combined.

> Pie Town, New Mexico, is actually named in honor of the apple pies produced by a general store built there in the 1920s. When the authorities urged the Pie Towners to use a more conventional name, they refused, and some ninety years later, they are still proudly holding annual pie festivals each September.

In 1934, Ritz introduced a recipe for "Mock Apple Pie," a combination of sugar, lemon, cinnamon, and of course, Ritz crackers, that imitates the taste and texture of a real apple pie.

As unappetizing as that sounds, it was popular during the years of deprivation during the Depression and World War II, and other mock dishes also took off. Mock maple syrup (brown sugar and water) and mock terrapin (chicken with eggs) were a few mock favorites.

APPLES

Each American eats an average of twenty pounds of apples a year. Germans eat an average of seventy-one pounds.

There are over one thousand apple varieties marketed in the United States. If you're feeling adventurous, put down that Granny Smith and try:

*King Luscious   *Maiden Blush
*Ben Davis   *New York 429
*Northern Spy   *Wealthy
*Westfield Seek-No-Further   *Hubbardston Nonesuch
*Summer Rambo (no relation to Sylvester Stallone)

When it comes to pesticide residue, apples are the most dangerous fruit. A survey by the anti-pesticide advocacy group Environmental Working Group found that apples, celery, and strawberries had the highest levels of pesticide residue when they got to the produce aisle.

On a positive note, the group also offered a list of least-contaminated produce. Onion, sweet corn, and pineapple topped the list.

BANANAS

Bananas can't reproduce. The beloved species of yellow fruit that holds a prominent place in supermarkets and fruit bowls everywhere, the Cavendish banana, is actually a seedless, impotent hybrid of two less appetizing plant species. Bananas have only been able to reproduce with the help of farmers, who remove and transplant part of the plant's stem.

This means we may soon be facing a banana apocalypse. Since the global cultivation of bananas has made them genetically identical to one another, bananas face increasing threats from pests and disease, which constantly evolve while bananas remain reliably, and maladaptively, the same. Researchers believe that within decades the Cavendish may no longer be viable for mass cultivation. So, enjoy that banana while it lasts.

Banana peels make great water filters. An environmental chemist in Brazil found that banana peels contain nitrogen, sulfur, and carboxylic acids that bond to the heavy metals polluting water around industrial plants. Tossing a bunch of dried peels into Brazil's copper- and lead-polluted Paraná River worked better than all the other filtering materials tested.

BEER

Brown bottles are better for beer than green or clear ones. Particularly for stouts, bocks, and other dark beers, the brown bottles protect the beer from the sun and other light exposure that can cause them to become "light-struck" (i.e., skunky). Since lighter beers absorb less sun than darker ones, it's usually not a problem to keep them in clear bottles—but for the best beer protection, go brown.

"Cenosillicaphobia" is the fear of an empty glass.

Your body can break down about 0.5 ounces of alcohol per hour—about the amount found in can of beer. Five percent is processed through the kidney as urine, another five percent is exhaled through the lungs, and the rest is broken down into acetic acid through the liver.

CHOCOLATE

Chocolate is better than kissing. In a test done by Mind Lab, eating chocolate caused the twenty-something volunteers' hearts to pound and brains to be stimulated longer and more intensely than when they kissed.

The word "chocolate" comes from the Aztec word *xocolatl*, which means, "bitter water."

Chocolate is something of a miracle food, when enjoyed in small doses. Studies have found that regularly eating small portions of dark chocolate can lower low-density lipoprotein (LDL) cholesterol, depression, and the risk of heart disease, cancer, and strokes.

Richard Cadbury invented the first heart-shaped box of chocolates in 1861.

COFFEE

Outside of those pesky palpitations, coffee may actually help your heart. A study of more than 37,000 people found that those who drank two to four cups of coffee a day had a 20 percent lower risk of heart disease than those who did not. Though tea drinkers may have an even greater advantage: those who drank three to six cups of tea were 45 percent less likely to suffer coronary problems. So, drink up!

> Legend has it that coffee was first discovered by an Ethiopian goatherd named Kaldi. Wondering why his goats were so jumpy after eating the red cherries on a nearby bush, he tried it himself, and the rest is history.

England's King Charles II banned coffee houses in 1675, worried that they had become meeting places for citizens to plot against him. The proclamation was rescinded the following year.

Americans originally bought their coffee beans green and did their own roasting and grinding. Folgers Coffee changed all that when it began offering coffee ready to brew.

Coffee is the second-most-traded commodity in the world. Crude oil is the first.

George Washington invented instant coffee. Not *that* George Washington—a Belgian man with the same name developed the hit product in 1909.

COOKIES

Fortune cookies were either invented in San Francisco or Los Angeles, depending on whom you ask. But they were certainly not invented in China, and restaurants there still do not serve them.

> *Sesame Street*'s Cookie Monster was originally named Sid.

The current best-selling type of Girl Scout Cookie is Thin Mints, with 25 percent of total sales. After Thin Mints come Samoas (19 percent), Tagalongs (13 percent), Do-Si-Dos (11 percent), and Trefoils (9 percent).

CUPCAKES

Before muffin tins, cupcakes were often baked in individual pottery cups and even teacups. Some believe this is where the "cup" in "cupcakes" came from.

⊨

GourmetGiftBaskets.com broke the record for the world's largest cupcake in 2009, defeating the existing 151-pound record-holder with a 1,224-pound, two million-calorie, pink cupcake. The bakers' original goal had been a 7,000-pound cupcake, but the weight of the expanding batter crushed one of the huge oven's convection tubes during baking.

⊨

Everyone knows "cupcakes," but less familiar are "cup cakes," traditional pound cakes with recipes as easy to remember (and measure) as 1, 2, 3, 4: 1 cup butter, 2 cups sugar, 3 cups flour, 4 eggs. It's also known as the 1234 Cake.

⊨

Neiman Marcus began selling "Cupcake Cars" in 2009. Equipped with a 24-volt battery, each one looks like a giant cupcake on three wheels and can go up to seven miles per hour. The bad news: they cost $25,000 each and only fit one person. The good news: you can customize it to your favorite color!

DOUGHNUTS

An American shipman named Hanson Gregory claimed to have invented the doughnut's now classic ring shape in 1847. At the time, most people prepared doughnuts in a diamond or twist shape, which ended up frying the edges and leaving the dough in the center raw. The ring shape solved this problem.

The first recorded use of the word "doughnut" is found in Washington Irving's *A History of New York,* from 1809.

ENERGY DRINKS

Energy drinks may be a gateway drink to alcoholism. College students who regularly drink highly caffeinated energy drinks are found to be at a higher risk of becoming alcohol dependent. In one study, those who had consumed a Red Bull or Monster at least once a week during the previous year also drank about 40 percent more booze than their less energized peers.

Your car can run on Four Loko. When the FDA banned drinks like Four Loko, which combine caffeine and alcohol, wholesalers began sending truckloads of the drinks to environmental services plants, where the alcohol is distilled and recycled into ethanol.

FAST FOOD

When McDonald's stores began opening in Germany, the original home of the Hamburg steak, the older generations protested. Eating with one's hands was considered rude, and conservative Germans were concerned that "fast food" would break up family mealtimes.

><ins>
</ins>

> For every grocery store in America, there are five fast food joints.

While California is the birthplace of fast food, including chains like McDonald's, Carl's Jr., Taco Bell, and Jack in the Box, it is now one of the states with the lowest levels of fast food consumption.

Thinking about fast food makes you work faster. At least that was the case for a group of college students who were asked to read a page of text after some were exposed to images of fast food logos and others weren't. The ones who saw the logos read 20 percent faster.

FATTY FOODS

The brain responds to fatty foods much like it does to marijuana. Burgers, fries, and the like release "endocannabinoids," which create the feeling of being high and trigger a desire to eat more high-fat foods. Munchies can give you the munchies.

FISH

That fish you just bought may be an imposter. Researchers have found 20-25 percent of the fish sold in Europe and North America is purposely mislabeled.. "Mahi-mahi" is often actually yellowtail, Nile perch is labeled as shark, and the mild tilapia is used to impersonate almost any fish. Red snapper, grouper, wild salmon, and Atlantic cod are believed to be the most likely to be fraudulent. Fishmongers have trouble discerning which fish is which when their scales and fins have been removed, so fish fraud runs rampant.

A can of tuna is great for your eyes. Tuna and other fish high in Omega-3 fatty acids have been found to reduce the risk of "age-related macular degeneration" (loss of vision usually caused by old age) in women.

FRUITS

> Biologists define fruits as the sweet ovary of a seed-bearing plant, which technically means string beans, corn kernels, and jalapeno peppers could all be considered "fruits."

GARLIC

Garlic actually attracts vampires. Well, the closest thing to vampires science can find: leeches. An experiment conducted by *Discover Magazine* found that leeches attach themselves to a hand smeared in garlic in just 14.9 seconds, compared to 44.9 seconds to a hand without.

⊨⊨

But aphids hate garlic. Spritzing plants with a concoction of crushed garlic and water is recommended for keeping the pests away.

⊨⊨

April 19 is National Garlic Day.

HAMBURGERS

The name "hamburger" comes from the port town of Hamburg, Germany, where the recipe of ground beef, minced onions, and seasoning called the "Hamburg steak" was developed.

Before there were Freedom Fries, we had "Salisbury steak." During World War I, patriotic attempts to remove German words from the English language led to hamburger's name change. It was named after Dr. James Salisbury, an advocate of eating hamburger three times a day and limiting intake of vegetables, fruits, and starchy foods.

The question of who first put the burger on a bun remains hotly debated, but the Cattlemen's Beef Board holds that café owner Fletcher Davis invented the hamburger in the 1880s. He sold the ground steak on two slices of bread, with mustard, mayo, onion, and pickles at his restaurant in Athens, Texas, and brought it to the world's attention at the 1904 St. Louis World's Fair.

HONEY

Bears do eat honey, but they are more often interested in the bee larvae found in the hives.

Honey is good for burns. New Zealand scientists have found that putting honey on a moderate burn eases the pain and promotes healing better than traditional gauze or dressings. Honey's antibacterial qualities create a favorable environment for healthy new tissue to grow. It also beat out the gauze and dressings in nine out of ten taste tests.

Scientists have also found that Manuka honey (from tea trees in New Zealand) helps fight the often deadly Methicillin-resistant Staphylococcus aureus (MRSA) bacteria, at least in a petri dish. When diluted, it produces the antimicrobial substance *methylglyoxal*, which makes MRSA more sensitive to antibiotics and easier to kill.

ICE

Craving ice is a symptom of anemia. People suffering from an iron deficiency often find themselves compulsively eating ice (a practice called "pagophagia"), which can cool off inflammation in the mouth brought on by the condition

KETCHUP

Ketchup likely originated in China as a boiled-down brine of pickled fish called ke-tsiap. Early western ketchups were made with mushrooms, oysters, and walnuts before tomato juice was introduced as the main ingredient.

While mango and raspberry salsas proliferate, you won't find fruit-based ketchups in U.S. grocery stores. The Food and Drug Administration's "standards of identity" legally require that ketchup include a combination of one or more tomato products.

☒

In 1998, psychologist Donna Dawson asserted that "Every choice we make and every action we take concerning food will say something about us," including how we use ketchup. She developed a Ketchup Personality Test, identifying seven "sauciological" categories:

- Dunking or dipping fries into a pool of ketchup: Methodical, tidy and trustworthy, but also a bit controlling

- Splodging sauce into the middle of the fries: Opinionated and ambitious

- Squirting and swirling sauce in thin lines: Lively, with active imagination, but often impatient

- Dotting ketchup onto fries: Amiable and friendly, but lives conservatively

- Drowning the food with the sauce: Noisy, brash, and the life of the party

- Drawing faces and words: Artistic and easygoing

- Containing ketchup in a separate cruet rather than on the plate: Outwardly charming, but snobbish, shallow, and materialistic

> Heinz added the "57 Varieties" tagline to its labels in 1896 to signify the variety of products it offered. At the time, the company actually offered more than 60 products, but Henry John Heinz liked 57; five was his lucky number, and seven was his wife's.

The Heinz Ketchup label featured a gherkin pickle for some 110 years, even though no pickles are included in the recipe. Looking for something simple to get his product noticed, H. J. Heinz gave away "pickle pins" at the 1893 Chicago World Fair, and the image stuck. In 2009, the company finally replaced it with a tomato.

LUNCH

The first character-licensed lunchbox came out in 1935 and featured Mickey Mouse.

For decades, almost all lunchboxes were metal. This changed in the 1970s when plastic lunch pails were introduced, not only because plastic costs less, but also because parents were worried that kids might use the metal boxes as weapons against other school children.

Parents still have reason to worry about their kid's lunch. A study of packed lunches at nine daycare centers found that more than 90 percent of the perishable items were at temperatures that invite germs. Even those parents who took precautions fell short, as only 14 of the 618 "ice packed" items still maintained safe temperatures by lunchtime. And who knows what germs those scientists digging through the kids' lunches were carrying?!

MEAT

Cold cuts are safer when they're hot. The Center for Disease Control and Prevention recommends that seniors, pregnant women, and those with weak immune systems avoid lunchmeats, hot dogs, and deli meats unless they are heated to at least 165 degrees. This kills the food-borne bug *Listeria monocytogenes*, which infects 1,600 people and kills 260 in the United States annually. Who doesn't like some hot bologna now and then?

MELONS

Cantaloupe is also known as rockmelon.

It's a healthy idea to wash your melons. While rinsing apples, peaches, and other produce where we eat the skin seems obvious, public health agencies also recommend washing cantaloupes, lemons, and other fruits and vegetables whose rinds we would never think of chewing on. The reason is that the knife used to cut into the produce can transfer the germs from the outside of the fruit into the delicious interior, which can lead to nasty diseases like listeriosis if ingested.

MILK

Scientists in China are engineering cows that can produce milk similar to human breast milk. By introducing human lysosome genes and other proteins into cattle embryos, they can produce milk that's easier for human babies to digest. Okay, but if they start teaching cows to sing lullabies, it's gone too far.

Water-buffalo milk contains less water than cow, goat, or sheep milk.

MUSTARD

Yellow mustard is produced from white mustard seeds (the color comes from adding spice: turmeric). Dijon and other spicy mustards come from brown and black mustard seeds.

Mustard seeds contain high levels of antioxidants, possess anti-bacterial properties, and reduce blood pressure.

But some put even more faith in the healing power of the plant. In the 1930s, London's Dr. Edward Bach asserted that the cheerful yellow mustard flower could cure gloominess. In the 1980s, mustard was the main ingredient of U.S. Patent No. 4428933, a product to treat acne.

While the coarse and spicy stuff proliferated throughout Europe, mustard did not take off in America until the R. T. French Company introduced its bright yellow, creamy French's Mustard at the 1904 World's Fair. It was a hit at the fair, and has since become the world's best-selling mustard.

The National Mustard Museum in Middleton, Wisconsin, features more than 5,300 mustards, a tasting bar, and the "Mustard-piece Theatre," which screens videos about how mustard is made.

The French currently use the most mustard in the world, about a pound and a half per person each year.

PORK

You think Americans like their bacon? According to the USDA Census of Agriculture, the top five pork-consuming countries are:

1. Denmark
2. Spain
3. Hong Kong
4. Germany
5. Hungary

POTATO CHIPS

Joseph "Spud" Murphy produced the first flavored potato chip in the late 1950s. His Cheese and Onion crisps were an instant hit and paved the way for BBQ, Cool Ranch, and Sour Cream & Onion flavors.

Potato chips are the cause of more weight gain in America than any other food including soda, candy, and ice cream. A Harvard University study of more than 120,000 people found that potato chips were responsible for an average weight gain of 1.69 pounds over four years. This was followed by potatoes (1.28 pounds), sugar-sweetened beverages (1.00 pounds), and unprocessed red meats (0.95 pounds).

POULTRY

When it comes to food poisoning, poultry is Public Enemy Number One. The University of Florida Emerging Pathogens Institute ranked the top sources of food-borne illness, and poultry contaminated with *Campylobacter jejuni* bacteria took the top spot, putting nearly 7,000 Americans in the hospital each year and costing $1.3 billion.

Pork contaminated with *Toxoplasma gondii* ranked a distant second (it hospitalizes 2,000 people per year), followed by deli meats tainted with *Listeria* (600 hospitalizations per year).

SALT

Americans consume the same amount of salt as they did 50 years ago, about 3,700 milligrams of sodium per day. The good news is that it hasn't gone up. The bad news is that the U.S. Department of Health and Human Services recommends no more than 2,300 milligrams per day.

The phrase "worth one's salt" refers to the currency in which Roman soldiers were paid.

Romans were also the ones who started the superstition that it was unlucky to spill salt (there goes your paycheck), which was also seen as an emblem of purity. In Leonardo Da Vinci's *The Last Supper*, an upturned saltshaker can be spotted on the table in front of Judas Iscariot.

Jungian psychologist Ernest Jones believed people love salt for subconsciously sexual reasons. For example, ancient Egyptian priests who abstained from sex also refused salt. The word *salacious* comes from the Roman word *salax*, meaning a man in love or in a "salted state." Also, salt is a major component of semen.

Salt is the only rock eaten by humans.

The white crystals have plenty of uses beyond flavor. A paste of salt mixed with flour and vinegar restores brass. Combined with turpentine, salt can restore shine to bathtubs and toilets, and warm saltwater keeps wicker from yellowing.

SANDWICHES

Sloppy Joes became popular during World War II when meat was carefully rationed—partly because it was easy to add fillers, like breadcrumbs, tomato paste, and onions that would make it last longer.

Peanut butter and jelly sandwiches became a hit for economic reasons as well. The high protein content and low cost of peanut butter made it a popular choice during the Great Depression, and it has since held on to its hallowed place among snackers everywhere.

Between the 1930s and 1950s, BLTs often included cheese.

SPICY FOOD

Man is the only animal that likes spicy food.

People in Buffalo, New York, call buffalo wings "chicken wings."

The hottest pepper in the world is the Bhut Jolokia, from Assam, India. Researchers at New Mexico State University determined it reaches one million units on the Scoville scale, which measures level of spiciness. The reigning pepper before Bhut was the Red Savina, which measured a mere 577,000 on the Scoville.

Spices may also fight colon cancer. Patients taking regular doses of curcumin (found in turmeric, a main ingredient in curry) and quercetin (an antioxidant found in onions) have seen as much as a 60 percent drop in the number of cancerous polyps on their digestive tract.

SUGAR

Sugar cane is a member of the grass family.

When sugar first reached Europe from Southeast Asia, it was a rare luxury. Generally, only royalty could afford to use it, considering that one teaspoon cost the equivalent of $5 today. It costs less than a penny now.

Our love of sugar has only grown sweeter with time. In 1884, the average American consumed 38 pounds of sugar a year. In 2001, this was up to 147 pounds.

Almost 60 percent of America's sugar production comes from beets.

VEGGIES

Eating vegetables can give you a tan. Researchers at the University of Nottingham have found that people who ate five additional portions of fruits and vegetables each day for two months saw their skin take on a more "golden tone." So, skip the tanning salon, and hit the produce aisle.

WHISKY

In Gaelic, "whisky" translates to *uisge beatha*, or "water of life."

At any given time, there are about 18.5 million barrels of whisky maturing in casks throughout Scotland.

CHAPTER 2

LOVE & SEX

What you never learned about the birds and the bees

AROUSAL

"Guys nights" may be key for men's erectile health. Researchers at the University of Chicago and Cornell University found that when a woman forms strong friendships with her partner's male friends, he is much more likely to suffer from erectile dysfunction. Time to take that boys-only trip to Vegas.

According to researchers, the Valentine's Day staples of choc-olate and wine do nothing for arousal. But saffron and ginseng boost sexual desire. So, for a truly romantic gift, go for the heart-shaped box of ginseng.

ATTRACTION

Happiness is not that sexy. A study by the University of British Columbia asked men and women to rate their attraction to hundreds of images of the opposite sex in different emotional states—shame, pride, happiness, and more. Women were least attracted to smiling, happy men and more attracted to those who looked proud or moody.

Gender equality leads to more sex. People in societies where women and men are seen as equals have more sex partners, more casual sex, and a greater tolerance and approval rate for premarital sex than societies where a gender gap persists.

As it happens, the countries with the highest levels of gender equality, according to the 2006 World Economic Forum's Global Gender Gap Report, are Sweden, Norway, Finland, and Iceland. And you thought it was the cold weather that made the Scandinavians frisky. By comparison, the U.S. came in a slightly disappointing 23rd place.

BACHELORS

James Buchanan is the only lifelong bachelor to be elected president of the United States. His orphaned niece, Harriet Lane, took on the hosting and other duties of the First Lady. Grover Cleveland was also a bachelor when he was elected in 1885, but he married over a year later in a ceremony at the White House.

Other famous bachelors: Ludwig Van Beethoven, Henry David Thoreau, and George Washington Carver.

BEAUTY

Plastic surgery is not just for the ladies. According to the American Society of Plastic Surgeons, men underwent 1.1 million cosmetic surgery procedures in 2010—up 2 percent from the previous year. Facelifts for men (up 14 percent) were the biggest source of this increase. The second? Cosmetic ear surgery (up 11 percent).

There is such a thing as beauty sleep. In a Swedish study, participants were shown two photos of each of 23 young men and women, one taken after eight hours of sleep and another after they stayed awake for 31 hours. They wore no makeup, were the same distance from the camera, and made the same expression, but the well-rested image was consistently selected as looking more attractive and healthier.

BIRTH CONTROL

Scientists have developed a birth control method for men. The injectable contraceptive, tested by the National Research for Family Planning in Beijing, is 99 percent effective by disrupting the hormones involved in sperm production. It may be just a matter of time before "Condom in a Syringe" hits drug stores.

BREAK UPS

A study of more than 10,000 Facebook status updates found that the most breakups occur just before spring break and just before Christmas. Happily, the day with the fewest number of breakups is Christmas Day.

Heartbreak should be called heart *brake* instead. Studies have found that someone's heart rate falls when they anticipate another person's opinion of them, and falls even further if they learn that the other person doesn't like them, before returning to its normal rate.

BREASTS

The average bra size in the United States is 36DD. Ten years ago it was 36C.

The bra market took off in 1917 when the U.S. War Industries Board called on women to make the switch from corsets in order to save metal. This freed some 28,000 tons of metal, or enough to build two battleships.

Humans can grow extra breasts. Areola, nipple, and breast tissue has been found on patients' backs, shoulders, faces, and thighs due to something called "pseudomamma." In 2011, a 22-year-old woman was found to have a nipple complete with a base of fat tissue, on the bottom of her foot. It gives "foot fetish" a whole new meaning.

CHEATING

Half of heterosexual men would forgive their partner for infidelity if it were with another woman. Only 22 percent said they would be forgiving if the woman cheated with a man. The opposite was true for women, where 7 percent were more likely to forgive heterosexual than homosexual cheating.

⋈

Powerful women are as likely to cheat as men. While guys usually hold the dubious distinction of being most likely to have an affair, women in positions of power and influence in their work are just as unfaithful as men.

CONDOMS

Two condoms are less safe than one—friction between the condoms makes them more likely to tear. They may also bunch up, making them more likely to slip off.

⋈

Ukrainian scientist Grigoriy Chausovskiy invented a musical condom. The device plays a different song depending on the couple's lovemaking position.

DATING

Rabbi Yaacov Deyo invented speed dating in 1999. Or rather, he popularized the longtime Jewish tradition of chaperoned gatherings of Jewish singles, introducing it outside of Judaism.

⋈

Women speak in higher-pitched voices to men they find attractive.

Technology is bringing people closer together . . . in bed. Almost 40 percent of women say that social media, including text messaging and Facebook, has led them to jump into bed with a partner faster than they would have before. According to a survey by *Men's Fitness* and *Shape* magazines, this is because it creates the impression of having known someone for a longer amount of time.

EXES

Women are more likely to dream about ex-boyfriends when they are ovulating. Researchers have found that women in long-term relationships have sexual desire for men other than their partner as they approach ovulation. So, if you're daydreaming about that biker dude from college, you might want to wait a week before giving him a call.

HORMONES

Women's tears reduce men's testosterone levels. A study by Israeli scientists found that women's tears emit chemical signals that are a hormonal turn-off for men. It's nature's way of saying, "Not now, honey."

Male testosterone levels also respond to the scents produced by women during ovulation. Researchers had men sniff a plastic bag with one of three shirts in it: a shirt worn by a woman who was ovulating, one worn long after she had ovulated, and one never worn by anyone. Testosterone levels dropped upon smelling the non-ovulation or unworn shirts.

KISSING

Kissing not only allows a partner to get a sense of their mate's hygiene habits, but also their DNA. Studies have found that women can subconsciously pick up on whether a man's genes are well matched to hers.

In longer-term partnerships, kissing continues to serve as an assessment tool for women, who use it to evaluate the state of the relationship. If a guy fails the kiss test, things could be headed downhill.

During a kiss, men pass along small amounts of testosterone in their saliva, which primes their mate's interest in sexual intercourse.

About two thirds of people tilt their heads to the right when kissing.

LOVE

True love is blind, or at least delusional. Psychologists have found that those who see their partner in simplistically positive and idealized ways, while overlooking negative qualities, have longer-lasting and more satisfying relationships. Romance is no place for realism.

⚏

In fact, love is kind of like cocaine. Feelings of head-over-heels romance activate the same dopamine centers of the brain that respond to drugs like cocaine or amphetamines. So, love has the same effect as a high-powered painkiller.

> Those looking for love might take a stroll to the local art museum. Blood flows to the pleasure center of the brain when a person looks at a painting they find beautiful, similar to what happens when you look at a loved one.

MASTURBATION

The word "masturbation" comes from the Latin roots of *manus*, meaning hand, and *stupare*, meaning to defile or dishonor.

During the mid-1800s, doctors tried to cure "hysteria" in women by inducing orgasm. A range of "cures" were devised to manage what was perceived as emotional excess in women, but French physician Pierre Briquet hit on a particularly popular solution when he introduced clitoral titillation as a way of calming hysteria. The doctor and patient would take part in therapeutic masturbation sessions, sometimes with a vibrator, other times manually. But the doctor would put a cover over his hand as he worked his magic, so it was totally not awkward.

ORGASM

Women can achieve orgasm through nipple stimulation alone.

Most of a woman's brain turns off during orgasm. Brain scans find that activity rises in one sensory part of the brain, but falls in areas involved in alertness and anxiety as a woman climaxes. But when women fake orgasm, the part of the brain controlling conscious movement lights up.

A similar study was conducted on men, but was considered unreliable. The PET scanners measure brain activity lasting more than two minutes—male orgasms usually don't last (quite) that long.

While 54 percent of women admit to having faked orgasm, 32 percent of men say they have as well.

For those women who have had no luck reaching orgasm, nerve specialist Stuart Meloy introduced his Orgasmatron in 2004. The small box attaches to the spinal nerves responsible for sexual pleasure via two thin wires, and by pushing a button, the wearer gets a powerful, completely real orgasm. The bad news? The Orgasmatron costs about $12,000.

PENISES

You know what they say about a guy with a big index finger . . . Korean scientists have found that penis size can be predicted by the ratio of the length of the index finger to that of the ring finger. The closer the two are in length, the larger the penis. This is not as random as it might sound: the level of prenatal exposure to sex hormones affects both the length of the two fingers and penis length.

Erectile problems? Eat some pistachios. Men who eat a cup of pistachios a day report a nearly 50 percent improvement in the erectile function questionnaire. Ratings of sexual intercourse satisfaction, orgasmic function, and sexual desire all rose steadily.

The size of a flaccid penis has no consistent relation to its erect length, which varies from less than a quarter inch to 3.5 inches longer.

You can break your penis. While no penis bone exists, "penile fracture" does occur, with an audible snap and plenty of pain.

As it happens, dissatisfaction with penis size is really a guy thing. Scientists who reviewed studies from the past 60 years found that 85 percent of women reported being happy with their partner's penis size. Just 55 percent of men said the same thing about their size.

RELATIONSHIPS

The longer you are in a relationship, the less you know about your partner. Research shows that members of younger couples who have been in a relationship just one to two years, are better able to rate their partners' preferences in food, movies, and kitchen designs than older couples that have been married for years.

But more older couples than younger say they are satisfied with their relationships. So it seems the key to a successful marriage is not paying too much attention to your partner.

SEMEN

Fatty foods can hurt your sperm. Men who eat foods containing lots of saturated fats—burgers, fries, etc.—produce fewer and less active sperm. On the other hand, eating fish or whole grains high in omega-3 and omega-6 fatty acids has been shown to create fit and plentiful sperm.

Men can be allergic to their own semen. It's rare, but a condition called Post Orgasmic Illness Syndrome can cause men to experience fever, fatigue, and burning eyes after ejaculating. The only treatment so far devised for this is exposing men to small amounts of their own semen and increasing the amount over time until they no longer react to it.

SEX LIFE

Age is nothing but a number when it comes to love. About a third of men older than 75 are still sexually active, including 1 out of 10 men aged 90 to 95. Now try getting *that* image out of your mind.

The number one cause of throat cancer isn't smoking—it's oral sex. The human papillomavirus, transmitted during oral sex, causes 64 percent of oropharyngeal cancers.

Sleeping around may be genetic. A scientist at Binghamton University has isolated gene DRD4 as a dopamine receptor connected to promiscuous behavior. Those with the gene have been found more likely to have one-night stands and affairs. So maybe you should give that cheating bastard a break . . . *nah.*

SINGLES

Researchers at the University of Chicago found that people find dates through friends and family twice as often as when they go to bars looking for love.

The highest single-woman to single-man ratio in the United States is in Florence, South Carolina, where there are just 68.97 men for every 100 women. The lowest ratio is in Jacksonville, North Carolina, where gentlemen outnumber the ladies by 174.78 to 100.

VAGINAS

The word "vagina" derives from the Latin word for "sheath, scabbard."

One of the latest beauty treatments is "vajazzling," in which women have tiny crystals placed in a pattern above their vaginas. Whether going with inexpensive plastic beads or high-end Swarovski crystals, these "labia sprinkles" have the dual benefit of making things look sparkly down there, and covering up any unsightly skin reactions from that Brazilian waxing.

The G spot is real—but not for everyone. In 2008, an Italian research team used ultrasound to determine that women with a thicker area of tissue between the vagina and urethra are able to enjoy G-spot orgasms, while those without the tissue do not. Of the 30 women tested, only 8 had G spots.

VALENTINE'S DAY

Valentine's Day actually honors three St. Valentines—a Roman priest, a bishop from Interamna (what is now Italy), and a Catholic saint, martyred in Africa.

The perfect lovers' getaway may be a tiny, uninhabited island in the center of the Adriatic sea that just happens to be shaped exactly like a Valentine heart. Formerly known as Galesnjak, it has since become more commonly known as Lovers' Island.

Deciding what to do for your partner on Valentine's Day? An online survey of more than 1,500 people found that most women found these to be the most romantic gestures:

1. Cover her eyes and lead her to a surprise (40 percent)

2. Whisk her away somewhere exciting for the weekend (40 percent)

3. Write a song or poem about her (28 percent)

4. Tell her that she is the most wonderful woman you ever met (25 percent)

5. Run her a relaxing bath (22 percent)

CHAPTER 3

FRIENDS & FAMILY

What you don't know about the people you know best

BABIES

Baby bottles could be making kids fat. Bottles have been linked to childhood obesity, with children who drink from them beyond age two more likely to be obese by age five. Scientists believe this may be partly because drinking calories is not as filling as eating them, so children can actually consume more than they need without feeling full. Or else parents are filling bottles with cookie dough.

Just to make all those new parents extra paranoid: pacifiers can cause speech impediments. A study in *BMC Pediatrics* found that preschoolers with speech disorders were three times more likely than other children to have used a pacifier for at least three years.

🦴

Babies blink less than adults.

🦴

Baby ads can be dangerous. More than one-third of the images of sleeping infants in women's magazines show the baby in an unsafe position, according to a study by *Pediatrics*. The advertisements and articles show babies nestled in loose bedding or on their sides or stomachs—positions that heighten the risk of Sudden Infant Death Syndrome. Just because it's adorable doesn't mean it's safe.

BIRTHDAYS

You are more likely to remember friends' birthdays when they are closer to your own. One study found the birthdays that subjects remembered were an average of 79 days away from their own, while those they couldn't recall were an average of 98 days away.

CHILDREN

Playgrounds may be too safe these days. Some psychologists believe that encountering risks (like 10-foot-high monkey bars or a steep slide) contributes to a child's development and his or her ability to face fears. Apparently, regulation and overprotection on the playground has led to higher levels of anxiety in younger generations. So go ahead and let little Timmy play on the rope swing.

Also, exposure to (some) germs at a young age can actually boost a kid's immune system over the long term. Research has found that kids are less likely to develop allergies, asthma, or autoimmune disorders as they grow up if they are allowed to get a bit dirty. Some researchers suggest this explains why girls—more likely to stay squeaky clean and away from germs—have a higher rate of asthma than boys (8.5 percent compared to 7.1 percent) and three times the level of autoimmune disorders.

Worrying has its advantages. A 90-year study that followed 1,528 Americans from childhood to old age found that those described as cheerful, optimistic, or worry-free, did not live as long as those who were described as worriers.

The belief that kids are more hyper after eating sugar is a myth. In a survey of 23 studies of sugar's effects on children conducted between 1982 and 1994, no discernable difference could be found between the energy levels of kids who were fed sugar and those who were not.

DADS

Becoming a dad reduces a man's testosterone level. Scientists believe this drop is an indication that mothers are physiologically meant to have help with childcare, and that men's bodies change in response to the requirements of fatherhood. Single men believe this drop is totally wimpy.

Thirty-something fathers are the happiest. According to research that looked at satisfaction levels in fathers going back 20 years, men in their 30s get more gratification and have more fun being a father than those in their 20s or age 40 and older.

Absent fathers cost the system $99.8 billion each year, according to the National Fatherhood Initiative. The cost of programs like child support enforcement, and social and health services for fatherless families can add up fast.

FAMILY MEALS

Eating meals together is not just good for family communication—it's good for kids' health. Combining data from

17 different studies, researchers found that children who joined in family meals were 24 percent more likely to eat healthy foods, 12 percent less likely to be overweight, and 35 percent less likely to suffer from eating disorders. Turns out "Eat Your Vegetables!" wasn't just one of mom's torture tactics.

> ## About 30 percent of the world's families eat with chopsticks.

Family meals can help you breathe easier. Research has found that kids suffering from asthma have better health when their families practice regular mealtimes during which parents show genuine interest in them. Meals with lots of disruptions (cell phones, television, etc.) and less interaction corresponded with poorer health.

⋈

Seeing pictures of comfort food actually comforts people. A study from McGill University found that men who looked at photos of meat on a dinner table became calm, even though researchers expected that it would make them feel more aggressive.

FAMILY SIZE

Honey, I shrunk the kids. In 2009, 58 percent of Americans said they wanted families of no more than two children—a big jump from just 17 percent who answered the same in 1960. Only about 33 percent think three or more children is ideal—down from 77 percent in the 1940s.

FRIENDS

You will replace about half of your friends in seven years. Social researchers have found that we regularly rotate the people we talk to about personal issues, pop in on for visits, and ask to help with moving and home repairs, cycling through a little over half of them in a seven-year period.

The United Nations set July 30 as World Friendship Day. In 1998, Nane Annan, wife of then UN Secretary-General Kofi Annan, dubbed Winnie the Pooh the world's Ambassador of Friendship at the United Nations.

We have fewer close friends today than 25 years ago. A study found that Americans' average number of confidantes slipped from three in 1985, to just two in 2011. A sad four percent of respondents reported having no close friends at all.

The size of your social circle may depend on the size of your brain. An Oxford scientist found that the size of an individual's "orbitomedial prefrontal cortex" (the part that assesses the moods and personalities of others) corresponds to the size of their social circle. Based on the average size of this prefrontal cortex, the typical person has 147.8 friends in their social network (no, not *that* social network).

 ## GRANDPARENTS

There are about 56 million grandparents in the United States.

☙

Grandparents are safer drivers than parents. Analysts of an insurance database found that accidents were twice as likely to occur when a parent was driving with a child than when grandma or grandpa was behind the wheel.

☙

Old people get a bad rap when it comes to driving. Younger drivers actually crash more often, due to the fact that they are more likely to speed or drive while intoxicated. But crashes involving the elderly are more likely to be fatal.

☙

In 1998, Italy became the first nation in recorded history with more citizens over the age of 60 than under the age of 20.

HOUSEHOLDS

More women live alone than men. According to the U.S. Census Bureau, 57 percent of those who live alone are women. This may partly be due to the fact that men live about five years less than women on average. The difference between the sexes: old and alone or dead.

More elderly parents and adult children are living in family homes today than in decades past. According to Pew Research's Social and Demographics trend report, multi-generation families increased 33 percent from 1980 to 2009. Economic challenges make it cheaper to keep ageing parents at home, rather than moving them into retirement homes, and cheaper for kids than getting places of their own. Parents have also gotten "much more chill" over the years, according to their twenty-something kids.

MARRIAGE

Women gain weight after marriage, and men gain it after divorce. A study of 10,071 people by Ohio State University found that women are more likely than men to experience significant weight gain during the first two years of marriage, taking into account factors such as pregnancy and socioeconomic status, while the same is true of men during the first two years following a divorce.

Marital satisfaction improves when children leave home.

Of course, there are worse situations than being fat and married—like being single (gasp!). Dozens of studies have found that married people tend to live longer than those who are single, so sociologists at the University of Louisville analyzed the data from 90 of these reports, which covered some 500 million people, and crunched the numbers. Their findings: Single men have a 32 percent higher risk of death than married men of the same age Single women have a 23 percent higher chance of dying than their married counterparts. So watch out all you bachelors and bachelorettes, your days are numbered.

On a kinder note: men get nicer after they get married. Nice guys may be more likely to get married in the first place, but studies have found that once married, men's antisocial behavior—such as breaking laws, failing to pay debts or acting aggressively—declines significantly.

Today, Americans are marrying later in life than they ever have, with the median age at (first) marriage 28.2 for men and 26.1 for women. In the 1950s, when marriage age was at its lowest, the median age at first marriage was 22.8 for males and 20.3 for females.

MOMS

Mother's Day was originally observed by members of women's peace groups and the mothers of soldiers who died in the Civil War. It was originally called "Mothers' Friendship Day."

Of women ages 40 to 44, about 82 percent are mothers. In 1980, a full 90 percent were moms.

Elizabeth Ann Buttle holds the record for the longest period of time between the births of two children. She gave birth to Belinda on May 19, 1956 and to Joseph on November 20, 1997, meaning the babies were born a whopping 41 years 185 days apart.

> Tuesday is the most popular day to have a baby. Tuesday's child is full of grace, after all.

OFFSPRING

Nuclear radiation leads to more baby boys. A study looking at gender statistics in areas affected by nuclear accidents in the U.S. and Europe found that populations exposed to nuclear radiation had unusually high rates of male births. Maybe that's why so many superheroes are men.

More Americans prefer sons to daughters. According to a Gallup survey, 40 percent of Americans said if they could only have one child, they would prefer a boy, while 28 percent said that about girls. This has changed little from the same poll that Gallup took in 1941, where 38 percent preferred boys to 24 percent who preferred girls. So there you have it: Americans are sexist pigs.

It's the men who get the credit for the phallocentric bias of the results. While the women surveyed were evenly divided on whether they preferred a boy or girl, the men weighed in with 49 percent for a son, and just 22 percent for a daughter.

PARENTS

Just 22 percent of parents say they are likely to spank their children for misbehaving, and 10 percent still use the paddle. The most common discipline strategies:

• Explain or reason with the child (88 percent)

- Take away a privilege or something the child enjoys (70 percent)

- Put a child in timeout, or grounding (59 percent)

⊨⊸

If parents only knew. While 52 percent of tenth graders in a survey reported drinking alcohol in the past year, only 10 percent of parents said they believed their child had enjoyed a drink. Researchers found an even greater disparity when asked about weed: Only 5 percent of parents thought their kids had smoked marijuana in the past year, though the number of tenth graders who admitted to smoking was closer to 28 percent.

⊨⊸

Parents who use a lot of "ums" and "uhs" when speaking to babies and toddlers may actually be helping their kids learn. As they try to understand speech, young children constantly predict what next word the adult will say. So, when parents fall into verbal fumbling (also called "disfluency"), it tips off young children that an unusual word is likely to follow, setting the stage for them to learn new information.

STEP FAMILIES

September 16 has been designated National Stepfamily Day.

TEENS

Most teenagers are liars. A survey of more than 43,000 teenagers revealed that 80 percent had lied to their parents about something significant within the past year. Not only that, 59 percent admitted to having cheated on a test, while 27 percent said they had stolen from a store. If you have a teenager in the house, go ahead and ground them—there's no doubt they've done something bad.

At the time of the Revolutionary War, more than half of America's population was 16 years or younger.

Teenagers today are more self-absorbed and angry—or at least that's true of their music. A University of Kentucky computer analysis of song lyrics from 1980 to 2007 found that the words "I" and "me" and anger-related words increased over time, while the words "we" and "us" and those expressing positive emotions decreased.

TODDLERS

You may be able to identify a future criminal as early as three years old. Psychologists in New Zealand tracked more than 1,000 children to identify connections between early behavior and their success as adults. Those who had trouble sticking with tasks, acted before thinking, and were generally restless and impatient were more likely to become single parents, be dependent on drugs or alcohol, and have a criminal record.

TWINS

In 2008, the birth rate for twins in the United States reached 32 twins per 1,000 live births—the highest on record.

> The West African tribe of the Yoruba boasts nearly 100 twins per 1,000 births, giving them the highest birth rate for twins in the world.

There were 44 pairs of twin girls given the names Ella and Emma in 2010, and 69 pairs of twin boys named Jacob and Joshua—making both pairs the most popular twin names for the year.

CHAPTER 4

MIND

Your brain's mysterious ways and waves

ADDICTION

Addiction to tanning is surprisingly widespread. One report from the University of Texas Medical Branch in Galveston found that as many as 50 percent of regular beach-goers qualify as having a substance abuse disorder, exposing themselves to ultraviolet radiation when they know it causes cancer. Those who tan 8 to 15 times a month reported experiencing withdrawal symptoms, including dizziness and nausea, when their tanning routine was disrupted.

Other odd addictions:

- Trichotillomania, or obsessive hair pulling, affects as many as 4 percent of Americans.

- Geophagia, the craving to eat dirt, coal, chalk, or clay, caused by nutritional deficiencies of iron or zinc.

- Some report tattoo addictions, whether from self-expression or as a way to soothe emotional pain.

*

Having trouble quitting smoking? You may first need to quit being impatient. A study from Oregon Health Science University found that 45 percent of smokers quit for good only after initially lapsing during the early weeks of cessation.

*

Destroying virtual cigarettes can ease nicotine addition. A virtual reality game in which subjects crushed as many cigarettes as possible for half an hour a week over three months led to 15 percent of them kicking the habit. So sometimes video games *can* be good for kids.

*

File this under "Just Can't Win." If a heavy smoker suddenly quits with little effort, he or she may have lung cancer. A study found that 48 percent of lung-cancer patients successfully quit smoking prior to being diagnosed with the disease, 31 percent without difficulty, and most not yet showing symptoms. Researchers believe this may be due to lung tumors that secrete a nicotine-blocking substance, decreasing the desire for a smoke.

ANGER

Psychologists categorize people as having three types of anger:

1. Hasty and sudden ("Hulk smash!"—Incredible Hulk)

2. Settled and deliberate ("I'll get you my pretty, and your little dog too" -Wicked Witch)

3. Dispositional ("Not my cup of mud"—Oscar the Grouch)

Venting anger does not actually get rid of it. Studies show that while throwing dishes or punching pillows might feel good for a moment, the more often you act on angry impulses, the more angry you will get next time something annoys you.

DAYDREAMING

Scientists refer to daydreaming as "stimulus-independent thought."

People spend 46.9 percent of their time thinking about something other than what they are doing. Hello? Are you paying attention?

That's too bad, because studies have also found that people are less happy when their minds wander, even when thinking pleasant thoughts. Apparently, there *is* something to those "live in the moment" inspirational posters.

Minds are most likely to wander while a person is resting, working, or using a computer. They are least likely to wander when they are making love.

DECISION-MAKING

Next time you get hauled before a judge, try to get in front of him as early in the day as possible. People who have to make frequent judgments tend to suffer what psychologists call "decision fatigue" the more choices they have to make. The later in the day, the more likely it is that a judge (or quarterback or business executive) will make dubious calls and demonstrate less than clear-headed judgment.

This also shows that sometimes it really is a good idea to "sleep on it" when a tough choice has to be made. Your decision-making ability will be much sharper at the beginning of the day.

DREAMS

Older people are more likely to dream in black and white. In one study, a quarter of those aged 55 and older dreamed in black and white, while only 4.4 percent of those under 25 did the same.

Smokers are much more likely to dream about smoking after they quit.

Seventeen percent of men have never had a wet dream.

EMOTIONS

Sure, Botox paralyzes parts of your face, but it may also make it harder to feel emotions. One study of 40 women found that after using Botox, it took them longer to process sentences conveying happiness, sadness, and anger. Scientists believe this is due to Botox inhibiting the cues that facial expressions send to the brain, making Botox users' minds as plastic as their faces.

Fake smiles are bad for your health. Slapping on your game face might help get through an awkward conversation or a dull meeting, but faking happiness takes its toll. Scientists tracked bus drivers, who are required to have frequent, friendly interactions throughout the day, and found that they tend to withdraw from their work while putting on a surface smile, and that by suppressing negative thoughts they actually made them more persistent.

FEAR

We may soon be able to erase our deepest fears. Scientists have found ways to destroy traumatic memories in mice by breaking down a molecular "net" in the part of their brain responsible for making and altering memories. The mice, which had been conditioned to fear a sound that preceded an electric shock, quickly forgot about the traumatic experience. Here's hoping they can do the same to my terrified response to hearing Black Eyed Peas songs.

The fear of fear is known as "phobophobia."

The fear of youth is known as "ephebiphobia." Sociologists point to it in explaining policies and behaviors that discriminate against the young by characterizing them as dangerous and destabilizing for society.

And one more: The fear of learning is "sophophobia." Hope learning that fact did not freak you out.

HAPPINESS

According to the Gallup World Poll, the United States is the 14th happiest country in the world. Respectively, the top five are Denmark, Finland, Norway, Sweden, and Netherlands (they seem to top every list, don't they?).

The unhappiest city in the country is Portland, Oregon—according to a 2009 survey by *Bloomberg Businessweek* that examined rates of depression, suicide, crime, and unemployment. It also included the number of cloudy days in a year (222 for Portland), which may have swayed the results. The full top five:

1. Portland, OR
2. St. Louis, MO
3. New Orleans, LA
4. Detroit, MI
5. Cleveland, OH

A similar study conducted by *CNBC* ranked the happiest cities as:

1. Boulder, CO
2. Holland and Grand Haven, MI
3. Honolulu, HI
4. Provo and Orem, UT
5. Santa Rosa and Petaluma, CA

Happiness is not good enough for most people. While humans enjoy the moment-to-moment joys of life, they will put up with plenty of drudgery for a longer-term sense of accomplishment, or what the psychologist Martin Seligman calls "flourishing."

INTELLIGENCE

Artificial flavoring might be making you dumber. A study of New York students found that those who avoided foods with artificial flavors and preservatives performed 14% better on IQ tests than those who stuck with the additives.

Time to rethink that "dumb jocks" stereotype. A raft of studies find that exercise builds neural connections in the parts of the brain responsible for memory and mental function. Increased levels of physical activity have also been associated with making kids more focused, earning better grades, and higher scores on standardized tests. Sorry fellow nerds, time to go for a jog.

MEMORY

Emotions outlast the facts when it comes to what we remember. Amnesiac patients were shown clips about death and loss from films like "Forrest Gump" and "Sophie's Choice." Five to ten minutes after watching them, the subjects could not recall what they had seen earlier, but retained a sense of the strongly negative emotions.

Booze keeps your mind limber. Studies show that having a few drinks a week increases the expression of the NR1 brain receptor that boosts learning and memory. A separate study found that seniors older than 75 who have about a drink a day are significantly less likely to develop Alzheimer's disease or dementia, according to research. Grandpa, that's *one* drink a day.

Watching someone else do something has been found to create a false memory of having done it yourself.

MIGRAINES

Looking at intense patterns, like high-contrast stripes or repeating, identical shapes, can trigger migraine headaches.

For that reason, scientists are developing special tinted glasses that can help migraine sufferers. The glasses, dyed in different comforting hues, normalize brain activity and comfort the wearer, reducing the occurrence of full-blown migraines. Apparently seeing the world through rose-colored glasses really can make life more enjoyable.

Bad headaches are good news for those concerned about breast cancer. Those who have a history of migraines are only 74 percent as likely to develop breast cancer as women who don't. Both diseases are influenced by hormonal changes, but scientists are not clear on the specific biological link.

POSITIVE THINKING

Repeating affirmations like "I am a lovable person" boosts the mood of people with high self-esteem, but makes those with lower self-esteem feel worse than they would have otherwise.

The candidate deemed to be "more optimistic" has won more than 80 percent of presidential elections, dating back to 1900.

POST-TRAUMATIC STRESS

Ecstasy alleviates post-traumatic stress disorder. A study of war veterans found huge drops in PTSD levels in those who took the drug compared to those who didn't.

PROCRASTINATION

Procrastination affects 25 percent of adults. I'm going to double-check that number tomorrow.

⊨

Research shows that intelligence has no correlation to procrastination. Though the act of putting things off has been found to decrease as we get older.

⊨

Procrastinators are less likely to put off work if they plan their play. Researchers have found that scheduling leisure activities made subjects better able to focus on their work and stick with it.

RATIONALITY

Men take greater risks than normal with their money when they're thinking about sex or romance. Women take fewer than normal.

⊨

Our greatest fear may be uncertainty. Scientists have found that the parts of the brain that produce feelings of fear (the amygdala and orbitofrontal cortex) are consistently more active when the stakes of a decision are unknown. Which might explain why, even though more people drown in the bathtub each year than suffer shark attacks, not too many people fear bathing (known as "ablutophobia," by the way).

We think we are spending less money when using credit cards versus cash. In one MIT study, students using a credit card for tickets to a Celtics game bid twice as much on average than those using cash.

REASON

Think there's a reason we seek "truth" and a need to more deeply understand our world? Social scientists writing in *The Journal of Behavioral and Brain Sciences* suggest that reason's evolutionary purpose is for winning arguments, rather than to refine our beliefs or to better understand the world. Watching cable news, I have to agree.

SPEECH

A rare medical condition known as Foreign Accent Syndrome causes sufferers to speak their native language in a foreign dialect, usually after a severe brain injury or stroke (or in at least one case, after dental surgery). Only about 100 cases have been documented since it was first reported in the 1940s.

Psst . . . whispering can be bad for your voice. Anyone who has suffered laryngitis has probably tried to "protect" their voice by whispering, but in fact many doctors and vocal coaches actually advise against this. Studies have shown that whispering does more damage to vocal chords than simply speaking softly. So, as our teachers reminded us during class, "No whispering!"

But humming is good for your sinuses. Keeping air flowing between the sinus and nasal cavities—which humming does better than almost anything else—helps ventilate and keep them clear of infection. Though it may not be good for the health of your relationships.

WILLPOWER

Having to pee increases your willpower. Studies have found that the more someone "holds it in," the more likely they are to give a correct answer to a question or make a responsible choice that will result in a greater reward for the long term. The same thing happened when people made a fist or flexed their biceps, with subjects showing more restraint than those who were relaxed. Performing a physical act of self-control triggers a mental state of self-control.

But willpower works the opposite way as well. Research has found that giving in to urges creates a domino effect of impulsiveness. Gratifying the desire for one type of reward, like food or sex, makes it more likely a person will give in to another urge, like gambling or impulsive shopping. For example, men with charged-up libidos are more impulsive when making financial decisions.

CHAPTER 5

BODY

The naked truth about your body's bits

BELLY BUTTONS

Belly buttons contain hundreds of bacteria strains, many of which scientists can't even classify. In a sampling from the belly buttons of 95 subjects, researchers found more than 1,400 bacterial strains, 47 percent of which could not be classified into any known family. The rest were different types of lint.

BLOOD

Donated blood is good for about 42 days.

The average amount of blood in an adult is 10 pints.

Your blood can tell your age. Blood tests are now available that can tell people their biological age, by measuring "telomeres," or structures on the tips of chromosomes that shorten the older people get. Cosmetic companies are expected to start selling telomeres extensions any day now.

BONES

> It is illegal to sell your own bone marrow.

BOOTY

Booty fat is healthier than belly fat. Extra weight in the thighs and lower body instead of around the gut actually indicates low levels of "bad cholesterol" and higher levels of the good kind that protects against hardened arteries. Researchers believe that having lots of gluteofemoral fat (aka "a big booty") may act as a buffer that draws in other fats that could have dangerous effects in other parts of the body. It also breaks down more slowly than belly fat, producing fewer chemicals linked to heart disease, diabetes, and obesity. So go ahead: turn around, stick it out. Even white boys got to shout.

BRAIN

Humans are the only animals whose brains shrink as we get older. And that is probably why the apes will one day rule us all.

〰

But one way to reduce this shrinkage may be exercise. A study published in the *Proceedings of the National Academy of Sciences* found that the hippocampus (the memory center of the brain that tends to shrink) in seniors actually grew 2 percent in those who walked three times a week or did toning and yoga exercises.

〰

The brain cannot feel pain. It may be the center of the nervous system that processes every itch, burn, or stubbed toe, but it has no sensory nerve system to detect any tissue damage, pressure, or discomfort.

〰

Scientists believe that ice-cream headaches, or brain freeze, result from the nerves responding to cold, causing blood vessels to constrict. When you breathe in, warm air causes the blood vessels to re-expand, which causes the intense headache. Some doctors recommend pressing the tongue to the roof of the mouth to warm the area in order to relieve the pain.

〰

The brain is the fattest organ in the body, made of about 60 percent fat.

All the computers in the world have about the same computing power as one human brain. According to a pair of researchers, the maximum number of nerve impulses a brain can execute per second is around 6.4×10^{18}—the same number of instructions mankind could carry out on all of their personal computers in 2007.

BREATHING

Breathing into a paper bag does not help hyperventilation.

DEATH

West Virginia holds the distinction of being the deadliest state in America, with 11.7 deaths per 1,000 people in 2009. Utah ranked the lowest, with just 5.1 deaths per 1,000 people.

The amount of energy required to cremate a body is equal to the fuel it takes to drive 4,800 miles.

For those who prefer to go out in a carbon neutral way, a process called "body liquefaction" may be a solution. The company Resomation began installing "alkaline hydrolysis units" into funeral homes in Florida: A body is submerged in a solution of water and potassium hydroxide, which dissolves body tissue, and then it's dumped into the municipal water system, and the bones are crushed in a "cremulator."

An American man's life expectancy in 2010 was 75.92 years and a woman's was 80.93 years. One hundred years earlier, it was 48.4 and 51.8 years old, respectively.

DISEASE

It's possible to get two colds at once. Colds come in almost 100 different strains, and when a person carries more than one strain at once, they link up and exchange genetic material, causing "co-infection" (aka "virus sex"). But there is no evidence that carrying more than one cold makes the symptoms any more severe or last any longer.

Only two diseases have ever been eradicated completely. The first is smallpox, stamped out in 1980 after an 11-year campaign. The other is . . . rinderpest, also known as bovine measles, which was just eradicated in 2011. Sure, you might think polio or malaria should be at top of the list, but these things take time.

EARS

Background noise makes food taste bad. Blindfolded diners tasted less sweetness and saltiness in the food they ate when white noise played than when it was not. This may explain why airplane food is so bland. Or so the airlines would like us to believe.

⟟

Smoking is bad for your hearing. In one study, young adult smokers had more trouble hearing extra-high frequencies than nonsmokers. In a separate study, those who were exposed to secondhand smoke were 1.83 times more likely to be unable to hear low frequencies.

⟟

A popular alternative medicine technique for "cleaning" ears involves placing a hollowed-out bee's wax candle in the ear. This "ear candling" is supposed to send smoke into the ear, creating a gentle suction that draws out toxins and earwax. Despite its popularity, most medical and health experts consider it ineffective, if not dangerous.

EYES

Babies don't shed tears until they are about eight months old. Their tear ducts have yet to fully develop and they produce just enough moisture to keep the eye hydrated.

Your eyeballs are directly attached to your brain, connected to a lobe responsible for sight information, located at the back of the head. While the other four senses send signals through networks of nerves, vision is a straight connection. If you opened your skull and removed your brain, the eyeballs would come with it.

FINGERS

Wrinkles form on fingers and toes when they soak in order to improve traction. Evolutionary neurobiologists believe that since the "pruney" wrinkles only appear on our digits that they are there to act like treads on a tire, creating better grip.

The *Oxford English Dictionary* lists seven names for the first finger on your hand (none of which is "pointer finger"):

* demonstrator

* forefinger

* index finger

* insignitur

* lickpot

* teacher

* weft finger

Fingernails take about six months to grow from base to tip.

Women have a finer sense of touch than men. In studies, women are able to consistently identify the directions of surface grooves more often than men. Researchers believe this has more to do with the fact that their fingertips are smaller than men's on average.

Manicures can be cancerous. The UV lights commonly used at salons have been linked to non-melanoma skin cancers on the hands of those who are regularly exposed to them. Since the lights give off UVA radiation, they work like tanning beds, with the rays deeply penetrating the skin.

HAIR

Going bald? Blame your lack of progenitor cells. This special type of stem cell, rather than testosterone, as it is commonly believed, appears to be responsible for male pattern baldness.

If you are going gray, you can blame pigment cells for slacking off. Hair-generating cells "ask" for hair pigment from pigment-producing cells, which send over the melanin. The amount of melanin determines whether you are blonde, brunette, or redhead. As the pigment-producing cells die off or are disrupted somehow, hair turns gray.

Scientists have found that bald men are at a higher risk for high blood pressure and heart disease than those with hair. We just can't win! What's next? America decides Patrick Stewart's no longer sexy?

♡ HEART

Heart attacks are 40 percent more likely to occur in the morning. The cardiovascular system follows a daily cycle, and there is more demand for oxygen in the first hours of the day, between 6 am and noon.

⊨⊣

In under a minute, your heart pumps blood to every cell in your body.

> Your heart pumps about 2,000 gallons of blood each day.

Heart disease actually kills more women in America than men. While the conventional wisdom may be that it's the guys whose hearts suffer the most, statistics actually find that some 500,000 American women die of heart disease each year—50,000 more than men.

A good song can be good for your heart. Listening to relaxing music has been found to significantly increase the dilation of blood vessels as endorphins in the brain respond to the pleasing sound. But music can have the opposite effect as well: In one study, those who were asked to listen to music they did not like actually experienced contraction in their blood vessels.

IMMUNE SYSTEM

Men are more susceptible to catching colds than women. Studies have found that men suffer more frequently and acutely from infectious diseases than women.

INTESTINES

You probably know your blood type, but what's your gut bacteria type? Molecular biologists have isolated at least three distinct "enterotypes," or bacterial communities in the gut that are specific to each person. You may be a *Bacteroides*, *Prevotella,* or *Ruminococcus* depending on which genus is dominant in your intestines. Not quite as clean as Type A or B, but then again, neither is your gut.

ITCH

One way to soothe an itch is with pain. Uncomfortable stimuli, including rubbing, heat, and electric shock have been found to wipe out itching sensations, and there is a negative correlation between pain sensitivity and itch sensitivity.

MEDICINE

You'd think most people would pay attention to what medicines they were taking—but you would be wrong. A survey of patients at a Colorado medical center found that they could not remember 60 percent of the medications that they had received while in the hospital. To be fair, a lot of medicines are really hard to pronounce.

"A spoonful of sugar" may make medicine more effective. Researchers have found that adding sugar to antibiotics kills the particularly tough-to-kill subset of bacteria called "persisters" that standard antibiotics have trouble reaching. Sweeter medicine may be on the way.

SNEEZES

Sneezes can travel at more than 100 miles per hour.

The practice of "blessing" someone when they sneeze goes back at least to ancient Rome. Pliny the Elder asked "why is it that we salute a person when he sneezes?" in his *Natural History* from 77 A.D.

In fact, not sneezing may be more dangerous than letting it out. Physicians warn that holding a sneeze in can cause everything from damaged eardrums, to nosebleeds to a detached retina. While these incidents are rare, the pressure created from a contained sneeze is not a force to be messed with.

You know that thing that happens when you glance at the sun and suddenly have to sneeze? Scientists have a name for it: an Autosomal Cholinergic Helio-Ophthalmic Outburst . . . also known as ACHOO. Seriously.

SWEAT

Women sweat less readily than men. In studies, they have to build up more body heat than men before the perspiration starts pouring.

TEETH

Occasional sugar binges are better for your teeth than small, frequent amounts of the stuff. Tooth decay occurs as simple sugars combine with the bacteria that line a person's teeth, creating acid that eats away at the enamel. This acid lingers for about 30 minutes, so continually sipping on a soda throughout the day is more likely to create cavities than having a quick drink at lunch.

TICKLES

It's impossible to tickle yourself. Researchers found that the cerebellum detects self-inflicted touch before it happens and alerts the rest of the brain to ignore the sensation. Go ahead and try it.

TONGUE

Your tongue is not mapped into distinct areas of taste. Though most of us learned in school that our tongues have taste receptors at specific locations (sweet on the tip, bitter in back, and so on), scientists have found that specific types of tastes are found in specific cells that are spread throughout the tongue. If this seems hard to believe, try finding the fifth basic taste, "umami" (or "savoriness," recently discovered) on a tongue map.

WEIGHT

Munchies aside, pot smokers are less likely to be obese than those who don't smoke. A study of more than 50,000 U.S.

adults found that while almost 25 percent of non-tokers were obese, the same was true of just 15 percent of regular weed smokers.

〰

Scientists have discovered the skinny gene. A particular genetic duplication makes men 23 times and women 5 times more likely to be underweight. The bad news? Chances are just 1 in 2,000 that you have it.

〰

Weight Watchers works better than doctors at getting overweight people to shed pounds. A study of 772 people found that those who were part of the weight-loss program dropped an average of 11 pounds over a year, while those who followed their doctors' advice only lost 5 a year.

WRISTS

If you had fat wrists as a kid, you might be at risk of heart disease. Scientists have found that large wrist circumference in children can indicate a resistance to insulin—an early sign of diabetes and risk of heart disease.

CHAPTER 6
WORK

On-the-job oddities

 ## BOSSES

Sarcasm from the boss improves worker creativity. Psychological research shows that people worked smarter, solving complex problems with more ingenuity, when a project was presented with a dose of sarcasm. The researchers found that the presence of anger in facetious comments helped focus the subjects' attention, while the teasing humor helped lighten it up enough to keep them motivated.

Each year, the organization eBossWatch gathers a panel of workplace experts to select America's Worst Bosses. The number-one worst boss of 2010 distinction went to Dallas Fire Rescue Chief Eddie Burns, whose sexual harassment lawsuits cost the city

$1.4 million in legal fees. Actor Steven Seagal ranked 46th after an assistant sued him for sexual harassment.

Nearly one-fifth of Americans think having an affair with the boss can lead to a better job.

While 7 percent of Americans say they have slept with their boss.

Frustrated with your boss? Better let them know. Men who are treated unfairly at work but do not express their concern have double the risk of suffering a heart attack in the next ten years compare to those who are more vocal, according to a study in the *Journal of Epidemiology and Community Health*. That does not mean shouting matches with the boss are an especially healthy idea.

BREAKS

A nap could save your life. Research finds that people who regularly take mid-day naps are 37 percent less likely to die from a heart attack or other coronary cause than those who work straight through the day.

Also, naps are a great way to memorize things. German researchers found that people who studied a set of cards and took a nap remembered 85 percent of the patterns. Those who didn't nap only remembered 60 percent.

Seventeen percent of Americans have had sex at work.

CALENDAR

> The 13th day of the month is slightly more likely to fall on a Friday than any other day of the week.

Though in Spanish-speaking countries, it's Tuesday the 13th that is believed to bring bad luck, as it was on a Tuesday in 1453 that Constantinople fell, ending the Byzantine Empire.

CO-WORKERS

Your co-workers may be killing you. A Tel Aviv University study of workplace conditions and health over a 20-year period found that those with less friendly colleagues were 2.4 times more likely to die during the study than those with workmates they liked.

Nice guys do finish last, at least in the workplace. Researchers find that workers with a high level of "agreeableness" on self-reported personality surveys earned an average of 18 percent less than those with below average agreeableness. Remember: When in doubt, be a jerk.

DESKS

The Equitable Life Insurance Company introduced the first "Modern Efficiency Desk" (aka the standard desk used by most workplaces today, with a flat top and drawers below) in 1915. It quickly became a workplace staple.

The Herman Miller Company introduced the cubicle in 1968. Cubes may now seem dull and uniform, but they were a big improvement for privacy and individuality at the time, compared to the massive open spaces with rows of desks that companies favored.

Robert Propst, the inventor of the cubicle, hated what his invention became. In 1997 he said that, "The cubicle-izing of people in modern corporations is monolithic insanity."

DIRTY JOBS

Some jobs can really be a bummer. According to a study by *Health* magazine, the fields where workers are most likely to be depressed are:

1. Nursing home and child care workers (11 percent reported a major bout of depression)

2. Food service staff (10 percent)

3. Social workers (10 percent)

4. Health-care workers (10 percent)

5. Artists, entertainers, writers (9 percent)

As bad as those numbers may look, the unemployed had it worse, with 12 percent reporting bouts of depression within the year—even the worst job is better than no job at all.

DISTRACTIONS

Surfing the Internet actually makes you a better worker. A study by the National University of Singapore found that subjects who broke up their work with periodic web-surfing sessions—

similar to taking a coffee break—were more productive than those who just stuck to their work.

similar to taking a coffee break—were more productive than those who just stuck to their work.

But this is not the case with other distractions, like emailing, texting, or making personal calls, all of which tend to require a full shift in concentration.

Workplace interruptions consume 28 percent of the workday, or $588 billion a year, based on an estimated average salary of $21 an hour.

The most distracting sound in the world may be whining. A study-group was challenged to try doing basic math problems while listening to a range of different noises. From a crying kid to a table saw, it was during the whining that the most mistakes were made.

> "Overhearing one end of a conversation is more distracting than hearing both sides."

DRUGS AT WORK

Food services workers are the most likely to use drugs or alcohol on the job, according to the Substance Abuse and Mental Health Services Administration. The organization surveyed employees and found the highest prevalence of on-the-job drug use in:

1. Food Services (16.9 percent used drugs or alcohol on the job)

2. Construction (13.7 percent)

3. Arts, Entertainment, and Recreation (11.6 percent)

4. Information (11.3 percent)

5. Waste Management (10.9 percent)

FEEDBACK

Getting fast feedback makes you perform better. Researchers at the University of Alberta found that subjects who had to make a public presentation gave stronger performances when they were told they would be getting graded right after speaking. When feedback was not promised, they did not do as well.

⊨⋲

But being told you are wrong increases stubbornness. Studies have found that people are less likely to change their minds when a large number of people disagree with them. In one test, subjects were asked to choose between two pieces of furniture, and after a break they were asked again, with the added information that a certain number of people preferred the item they did not choose. When a large majority preferred the item they didn't choose, the subject was more likely to stick with his or her original selection.

FUN

Joking around at the office has been found to improve creativity, cohesiveness among employees, and overall performance. That doesn't mean Xeroxing your backside leads to a promotion.

INTERVIEWS

Good looks are a good thing for men trying to land an interview, but not for women. A study in Israel found that when a résumé included a photo of a handsome man, that person was twice as likely to get a request for an interview than those with no photo and 30 percent more likely than plain-looking men.

⊨⊨

For women it was the opposite. The ones with no photo got the highest response, and the ones with an attractive photo received the lowest response of all. The researchers actually believe this may be due to the disproportionate number of young, single, women who did the resume screenings for human resource departments.

The New England Human Resources Association HR Network rates the top ten interview mistakes as:

*Being unprepared	*Lack of interest
*Inappropriate attire	*Lack of punctuality
*Poor body language	*Lack of résumé knowledge
*Unprofessionalism	*Rambling answers
*Use of cell phones	*Poor listening

 OFFICE SPACE

The largest "office building" in the world is the Boeing Everett Factory in Everett, Washington. Measuring in at 4.3 million square feet, the airplane assembly building has space to build Boeing 747s, 767s, 777s, and the new 787 Dreamliner.

The strangest office building may be the Newark, Ohio headquarters of the Longaberger Company, which manufactures handcrafted maple wood baskets. Its employees work out of an 180,000-square-foot, seven-story-tall replica of one of the company's baskets.

Getting an office with windows is good for more than just prestige. Studies have found that workers at jobs with little exposure to sunlight face a greater risk of kidney cancer, likely related to the decreased production of the cancer-fighting vitamin D triggered by ultraviolet light. So getting outside, or at least near a window, could save your life.

RETIREMENT

Retirement is also good for your health. Swedish researchers found that seven years after retirement, there was a 40 percent drop in depression among subjects, and an 80 percent drop in mental and physical fatigue. Why replacing work obligations with endless free time would put anyone in a better mood remains a mystery to the scientists.

Retiring at 65 is growing increasingly rare. The number of workers over the age of 65 rose by more than 21 percent between 1990 and 2000, even though that population only rose by about 12 percent.

SAFETY

The most workplace accidents occur on a Wednesday.

Fishing is dangerous. According to the U.S. Bureau of Labor Statistics, the fishing industry has the highest fatal work injury rate (116 fatalities per 100,000 workers). This was followed by logging workers (91.9 fatalities), aircraft pilots and flight engineers (70.6 fatalities), and farmers and ranchers (41.4 fatalities).

Ninety-two percent of workplace fatalities are male.

SALARY

The price of happiness is about $75,000. According to Princeton economists, that is where the rise of emotional wellbeing essentially stops rising along with income. At that point, for the average American, many stresses related to not having enough money have tapered off, but those earning beyond it do not show increasing levels of satisfaction. Who *wants* to be a millionaire?

SITTING

Want to improve your posture at work? Take a photo of yourself. Ergonomists have found that an exceptionally effective way to get people to stop slouching is to show them images of themselves seated at their desks.

Stand up and walk around. Right now. Taking breaks from sitting throughout the day, as short as one or two minutes, has been shown to reduce your waistline by a few centimeters and decrease levels of proteins that can lead to heart disease.

Just to give you an added scare: those who spent 10 or more years at a sedentary job—in other words, a "desk job"—had twice the risk of colon cancer and a 44 percent increased risk of rectal cancer compared to those who never held a sedentary job.

SMOKING

Smokers call in sick an average of 7.67 days more per year than non-smokers.

STOCK MARKET

At least twice, Nasdaq has been knocked out by squirrels. In 1994, it blacked out for 34 minutes when a squirrel chewed through a power line, and in 1987, a squirrel touched off a power failure that left Nasdaq without power for 87 minutes. This is what happens when squirrels try to invest all those nuts they've been saving.

STRESS

Loud noises at work can double your risk of heart disease. A study of more than 6,000 workers found that those who worked around loud noises (loud enough that they had to raise their voices to be heard) for at least three months were significantly more likely to suffer from heart disease. The noise increases the level of stress hormones like cortisol and adrenaline, creating higher risks of heart failure, strokes, or high blood pressure. So earplugs might be a worthwhile investment.

Working long hours increases your chance of heart disease as well. Men and women who work 10 hours a day or longer are at a 45-percent higher risk of a heart attack than those who work 7 or 8 hours a day. Those who work 11 hours or more are at a 67-percent higher risk.

The smell of an anxious person increases your level of anxiety. Subjects in a study were asked to smell the armpit sweat of college students generated both before they took a test and also during exercise. The anxious, pre-test sweat activated parts of the brain related to empathy in the smellers. Thinking about smelling dozens of people's armpit sweat is activating the revolted parts of my brain.

"Washing your hands" of a decision is not just a metaphor. People are better able to distance themselves from guilt or stressful feelings about difficult moral decisions, as well as bland everyday decisions, by physically washing their hands.

TYPING

The longest word that can be typed with just your left hand on a conventional keyboard is *sweaterdresses* (for those word nerds who cry foul that it should include a hyphen, the longest word is *stewardesses*). The longest word with just your right hand is *johnny-jump-up*, a type of European wildflower.

> *Typewriter* is typed with just the top row of keyboard keys.

Alaska is the only state name that can be typed with a single row of keys.

WORK SCHEDULE

Women are more likely than men to feel guilty about taking time off from work (40 percent versus 29 percent).

Eight-hour workdays? Ha! Americans spend an average of 3 hours and 58 minutes of the workday actually doing work, according to the U.S. Labor Department. Some of the activities we spend the rest of the day doing:

- Watching television: 2 hours, 31 minutes

- Leisure and sports: 2 hours, 9 minutes

- Sleeping: 8 hours, 23 minutes

- Personal care: 49 minutes

- Buying things: 43 minutes

CHAPTER 7
PLAY

Strange facts about hobbies, sports, and leisure

BASEBALL

The longest baseball game on record was between the Chicago White Sox and the visiting Milwaukee Brewers on May 9, 1984. The game went 25 innings and lasted 8 hours and 6 minutes.

⊨⊨

One of the earliest recorded uses of the word "baseball" appeared in 1803, in Jane Austen's *Northanger Abbey*. The first was a 1744 publication by children's publisher John Newbery called *A Little Pretty Pocket-Book* which includes a rhyme entitled "Base-ball."

⊨⊨

BASKETBALL

Nine of the ten largest high school gymnasiums are located in Indiana. The excitement around the high school basketball tournament in the state is unique in its intensity, and has been dubbed "Hoosier Hysteria."

BOATING

In April 2011, the U.S. Coast Guard had to lower the number of people allowed on ships because of how fat we've all gotten. The "Assumed Average Weight per Person" has been raised from 160 pounds to 185 pounds. So while a boat with a 16,000-pound capacity would previously have been allowed to carry 100 people, it can now only handle 86 of us. See what happens, America? You had to have all those cheeseburgers and now your yacht parties suffer.

BOREDOM

April 11, 1954, is the most boring day in history. At least according to software developers at True Knowledge, a search engine project that collects and organizes facts. Of the service's more than 300 million facts, a measly two occurred on 4/11/54: a Turkish academic named Abdullah Atalar was born, and a soccer player (that's a footballer to everyone outside of North America) named Jack Shufflebotham died. In the last 110 years, no other day was less interesting. With apologies to Dr. Atalar and Mr. Shufflebotham.

BOWLING

A bowling pin will fall at an angle of 7.5 degrees.

DANCING

Good dancing is all in the neck, torso, and right knee. Psychologists in the UK have found that women are most attracted to men who move their upper bodies, vary their dance moves, and take up a lot of space. Swaying hips don't make much of a difference either way.

DRINKING

Drinking doesn't hurt your test scores the next day. A study of 196 college students found that those who drank to a 0.12 percent blood-alcohol level and took multiple-choice tests the next day, performed just as well as those who abstained.

Though that might just be due to the test-takers' youth. Researchers have found that teens are able to shake off the immediate effects of intoxication and hangover better than older counterparts because adolescent brains are more resilient, even though drinking at a young age can cause long-term brain damage.

Almost one in four Americans has participated in binge drinking (defined as five or more drinks on one occasion).

DRIVING

Just 2.5 percent of people can use a cellphone while driving without negatively impacting either task. So, that probably doesn't include you.

FOOTBALL

The football went on a diet in 1934, when the heads of the NFL made it longer and skinnier.

The Baltimore Colts were the first professional football team to have its own organized cheerleading squad, introduced in 1960. It didn't take long for the other teams to follow their lead.

AstroTurf was first used on a major sports field in 1966, installed in the Houston Astros indoor stadium.

HORSE RACING

Only 11 horses have won the Triple Crown of the Kentucky Derby, Preakness Stakes, and Belmont Stakes.

⊨⊰

A horse cannot be registered as a Thoroughbred unless the actual mating between mare and stallion is witnessed. Artificial insemination doesn't cut it.

MEDITATING

Meditation makes an excellent pain killer. In studies where subjects' legs were poked with a hot probe, those who had studied Zen meditation for 1,000 hours had greater pain tolerance than those who had little meditation experience. The meditators could handle temperatures of more than 10° Celsius higher than the control group.

⊨⊰

Even casual meditators can handle more pain. In a separate study, subjects who had done about an hour and a half of "mindfulness meditation" training reported a 40 percent decrease in pain intensity and a 57 percent drop in pain unpleasantness (morphine only reduces pain by about 25 percent).

MOVIES

The first movie theater was Edison's Vitascope Theater, built in the Ellicott Square Building in Buffalo, New York. The

72-seater opened on October 19, 1896 using one of Thomas Edison's Vitascope Projectors.

〰️

The average movie ticket price in 1948 was 36 cents.

〰️

Psychology professors at UC Berkeley have decided that the saddest movie of all time is *The Champ*, starring Jon Voight. After a five-year study of how viewers responded to 250 different films, the professors found that subjects experienced high levels of sadness while watching it—higher than any other film. So, probably not a great date movie.

MUSIC

Loud music on headphones or at concerts can cause hearing loss, but playing music at a normal volume can actually improve your hearing as you age. Studies have shown that older musicians are 40 percent better at hearing sentences over noisy background environments than non-musicians. Similar to memory exercises, musicians regularly focus on small tonal details of sounds that non-musicians neglect, allowing them to better pick up on words and conversations as well.

〰️

But if you're using a brass or woodwind instrument, consider sterilizing it before putting it into your mouth. Researchers found 295 different bacteria, as well as yeasts and molds, on a sampling of

13 instruments from a high school band room. They warned that it could lead to infections in the mouth, or the gastrointestinal, and respiratory tracts.

OUTDOORS

A full 51.4 percent of Americans did not participate in outdoor activities in 2010.

According to the Outdoor Industry Association, the most popular outdoor activities in America are:

1. Running and Jogging (18 percent)

2. Fishing (16 percent)

3. Biking (15 percent)

4. Car Trips, Backyard, and RV Camping (15 percent)

5. Hiking (11 percent)

PARTYING

The greatest food fight on the planet may be La Tomatina, a party that occurs in late August each year in Buñol, Spain. Some 30,000 people descend on the small town to throw about 90,000 pounds of tomatoes at each other. While the only point of the festival is to have a messy good time, the city council does ask that tomatoes be squashed before hurling. Killer tomatoes could definitely ruin the fun.

〰

At Songkran, the Thai New Year celebration, water is the projectile of choice. Taking place over a sweltering weekend in mid-April, Songkran features Super Soaker fights, water tossed at images of Buddha in order to "bathe" them, and more wet t-shirts than you are likely to find at any beach during America's spring break.

〰

> Some other strange New Year Eve's traditions include:
>
> Wearing brightly colored underpants in Brazil
>
> Wearing polka dots and eating round fruits in the Philippines
>
> Burning effigies of celebrities and politicians in Panama
>
> Jumping off chairs at the stroke of midnight in Denmark
>
> Baking a lucky coin into a sweet bread in Greece

Despite their reputation, college students are not the hardest partiers in the country. That distinction goes to the urbane, affluent, recent college *graduates* whom the National Institute on Alcohol Abuse and Alcoholism have dubbed "Cyber Millennials." They may exercise, eat organic food, and generally avoid smoking, but they also binge drink more than any other demographic.

READING

We don't read letters from left to right. In fact, we read them in short chunks simultaneously. In tests where subjects were shown words quickly, then asked what they had seen, they had just as much trouble identifying the first letter of the word as the last. When they were given more time, readers became more accurate on all the letters, leading researchers to conclude that the letters were processed simultaneously.

Spoiler alert: knowing the end of a story doesn't actually spoil it. UC San Diego psychology researchers had 30 subjects read 12 mystery or surprise-ending short stories by authors like John Updike, Roald Dahl, and Agatha Christie. Some subjects received a spoiler paragraph and others did not. For all but one story (Anton Chekov's "The Bet" for some reason), respondents significantly preferred reading the story after already knowing how it ended.

RELAXATION

Resting in a hammock offers an easier, deeper sleep than resting in a stationary bed. Swiss scientists found that the rocking motion from a hammock caused nappers to fall asleep faster than when sleeping in a bed that did not move. But don't take their word for it, head out to the hammock and give it a test run yourself.

RUNNING

Forget about sports drinks, a study has found that beer is a great recovery drink for runners. Well, non-alcoholic beer (there's always a catch). Researchers at the Technical University of Munich found that runners who drank about a liter of non-alcoholic beer each day during marathon training showed less inflammation in their blood and lower white blood cell counts than those who drank a similarly flavored placebo. This is likely because the beverage contains loads of polyphenols, which help boost the immune system.

While regular beer has these polyphenols, the scientists believe the alcohol counteracts many of the positive effects of drinking so much of it. I'd be happy to help them test this theory.

SHOOTING

> There are 56 emergency room visits a day in the US due to injuries from BB and pellet guns.

SHOPPING

In-store music makes you spend more. While up-tempo music keeps crowds moving and mellow songs encourage browsing, a study by Texas Tech University found that playing classical music in a wine shop led shoppers to buy more expensive wine. They bought the same number of bottles when Top-Forty pop songs played, but bought the cheaper stuff. Like the old saying goes: don't go grocery shopping when you're feeling hungry or wine shopping when you're feeling classy.

The highest proportion of online shoppers is in South Korea, where 99 percent of Internet users have used it to shop. According to Nielsen, the U.S. is ranked eighth, at 94 percent of the population.

The most popular items purchased online are books, which 41 percent of shoppers said they purchased in a three-month period, according to Nielsen (second place was clothing and accessories, at 36 percent).

> Four of the ten largest shopping malls in the world are located in China. The world's largest is the 7.1-million-square-foot New South China Mall in the city of Dongguan, which includes its own windmills and theme parks, as well as a replica of the Arc de Triomphe.

Men are just as likely as women to be compulsive shoppers. A study at Stanford University found that the compulsion to go on shopping binges, purchasing unnecessary and unwanted items occurs in 6 percent of women, as well as 5.5 percent of men.

SUNBATHING

Flavonoids found in grapes can stop the chemical reactions that cause sunburn, premature aging, and skin cancer when applied to skin. But scientists have found no conclusive evidence that pouring a bottle of merlot on your head is a good pre-beach idea.

⌗

But a cup of iced coffee might be. Caffeine has been shown to help repair sun-damaged skin. Combined with exercise, the equivalent of two cups of coffee a day caused a 400 percent increase in the repair to cells damaged by UVB rays.

SURFING THE WEB

Surfing the Internet actually makes you smarter. Brain scans of people between the ages of 55 and 78 found that those who surfed the web for an hour a day for 7 days activated parts of the brain involved in decision-making and working memory, while those who skipped the surfing showed little activity.

SWIMMING

One in five Americans admit to peeing in the pool.

⌗

The deepest indoor swimming pool in the world is known as Nemo 33. Located in Brussels, the pool runs 113 feet deep (or 34.5 meters) and serves as a swimming pool, scuba training facility, and film set. The distinction of deepest *outdoor* pool is held by the San

Alfonso del Mar resort, which boasts a pool two feet deeper than the Nemo 33.

⌘

The local swimming hole may be a place of fond summer memories for most. For a rare few, it's a cesspool of deadly brain-eating amoebae. Each year, three or four people in the U.S. are killed by the single-cell *Naegleria fowleri*, which thrives in warm, stagnant water and can enter through a person's nose as they're jumping into the water or doing a cannonball (its victims are often exuberant children who forget to hold their noses). Once inside, it infects the victim's central nervous system, almost always resulting in death. The good news: chances of being infected are 1 in 10 million.

TELEVISION

Watching an hour of television can shorten your life by 22 minutes. Scientists at the University of Queensland in Australia studied some 11,000 people over the age of 25. The 9.8 billion hours the subjects watched collectively was associated with the loss of 286,000 years of life, or about 22 minutes less life for every hour watched.

⌘

For kids, it's even worse. Fourth graders who watched more television as preschoolers were more likely to be bullied, worse at math, and have a worse diet. For every hour a preschool kid watched in the average week, he or she suffered about 10 percent more teasing and harassment from fellow students. Except for those who just watched Chuck Norris movies—they took crap from nobody.

TOYS

The world's largest distributor of toys is McDonalds.

> LEGO produces more tires (306 million per year) than any other manufacturer in the world. Sure, they're toy tires, but still.

The first toy advertised on television was Mr. Potato Head.

Barbie and Ken were named after the children of the dolls' creator, Ruth Handler (their names were actually Barbara and Kenneth).

VACATION

In 2009, 34 percent of Americans did not use all of their vacation days.

The most popular vacation destination is France, where 79 million tourists visited in 2008. This is followed by the United States, Spain, and China.

⋈

While the U.S. may be only the second most popular country in which to vacation, it boasts four of the top five most visited tourist attractions in the world:

1. Times Square, New York City

2. National Mall and Memorial Parks, Washington, D.C.

3. Disney World, Orlando

4. Trafalgar Square, London

5. Disneyland, Anaheim

⋈

While 137 countries mandate paid vacation time, the United States is the only industrialized country that does not.

⋈

The Blarney Stone, which some 400,000 people have kissed for good luck, was named the most unhygienic tourist attraction in the world by TripAdvisor. The Market Theater Gum Wall in Seattle, on which tens of thousands of people have stuck their used chewing gum, received second place.

While Oscar Wilde's tomb in Paris received third place for the torrent of unhygienic lipsticked kisses left on the elaborate tombstone, it is sure to lose that dubious distinction soon. In November 2011, a glass barrier was installed to keep the dandy's romantic fans from leaving their marks.

⋈

A vacation could save your life. A study found that women who only take a vacation once every six years or less are nearly eight times more likely to have a heart attack or develop coronary heart disease than those who took at least two vacations a year.

WRITING

The dot above the letter *i* is called a tittle.

Before you start giggling, you may also be interested to know that the phrase "To a T" is likely a derivation of "To a tittle," meaning to the smallest detail—similar to the more common expression "Dot your i's and cross your t's." Okay, go ahead and giggle.

CHAPTER 8

AROUND THE HOUSE

The peculiar things happening in your home

BATHROOM

Thomas Crapper did not invent the flush toilet, despite the legend. Sir John Harrington invented it in 1596. But Crapper did popularize the toilet and even invented the ballcock used in flush toilets today.

Toilet paper was originally sold in packages of flat sheets. Rolled toilet paper was invented around 1880.

Being clean may carry dangers. Children and teens who use antibacterial soaps are at an increased risk for hay fever and other allergies. A person's increased exposure to chemical triclosan, used widely in soaps, toothpaste and medical devices, has been found to correlate with an increased likelihood he or she will be diagnosed with allergies.

November 19 was named World Toilet Day by the World Toilet Organization (yes, both those things actually exist). On a more serious note, the day was established to raise awareness of the 2.6 billion people who do not have access to clean, proper sanitation.

CHORES

Boyfriends do more housework than husbands. An international study of more than 17,000 people found that after marriage, the amount of time each week a man spends doing chores drops off considerably.

The husbands might want to get cleaning if they want to keep their marriage strong. A Pew survey of Americans found that 62 percent believe helping with chores to be "very important" to the health of a marriage—a 15-point jump from 17 years before. Only sex (70 percent) and fidelity (93 percent) received higher votes.

Be careful this winter: U.S. hospitals treat about 11,500 injuries and emergencies each year related to shoveling snow.

DOGS

Dogs can smell cancer. Researchers believe that a body that has developed cancer puts out a unique scent that dogs' sensitive sense of smell can detect. In one study, four family dogs smelled test tubes containing breath samples of 220 subjects and correctly identified 71 of the 100 of them who had lung cancer. In another study, dogs were able to identify the presence of early-stage polyps of colorectal cancer through 33 out of 36 breath tests and 37 of 38 stool samples.

Dogs were domesticated from gray wolves over a 15,000-year period.

The Wire Fox Terrier breed has won "Best in Show" at the Westminster Show 13 times, making it the highest-winning breed in the 134-year-old show's history. Labrador Retrievers and Golden Retrievers have never won.

DUST

Dust may actually help clean the air in your home. The dead skin cells we shed constantly that end up in dust around the house contain an oil, called squalene, that reduces indoor ozone levels as much as 15 percent. The squalene's molecules bond with the ozone and break it apart, making the air safer to breath. So skip the dusting for a day, it might actually make the house cleaner.

GARDEN

The oldest known garden gnome in the world is named Lampy, the last surviving lawn ornament from a set of 21 imported into England from Germany in the 1840s.

> The Garden Gnome Liberation Front has made a mission of stealing the statuettes from gardens in France, often leaving behind a note supposedly from the gnome himself explaining that he left because he felt he was disrespected. In 1997 alone, the group swiped more than 150 gnomes. More whimsical liberators take photos of the gnome in exotic locations and send them to the owner before finally returning him.

If you should find there is lead in your soil (from decades-old car exhaust or lead-based paint residue), you can neutralize it with fish bones. The calcium phosphate in the bones binds with the lead deposits and turns it into the harmless pyromorphite. It's likely cheaper than moving the mounds of dirt plus it gives you an excuse to eat all the fish and chips you want.

KITCHEN

> Hot water freezes faster than cold water. As it begins to evaporate, water loses mass, so it takes less energy to freeze.

Chewing gum after a meal can reduce the severity of heartburn. The saliva that chewing stimulates neutralizes the acid reflux, forcing them back down into the stomach. So skip the after-dinner mint and grab a stick of Trident.

In Scotland, griddles are often called "girdles."

Historians believe the oldest metal cooking utensil is the kettle.

LIGHTING

The world's largest crystal chandelier is kept in Istanbul's Dolmabahçe Palace. A gift from Queen Victoria, it has 750 lamps and weights a full 4.5 tons. Hopefully it's very securely fastened.

PETS

As America gets fatter, so do our puppies and kittens. By the end of 2010, about half of the country's domestic animals were overweight, according to the Association for Pet Obesity Prevention. One-fifth of dogs and cats are considered obese—usually from overfeeding. Time to buy that BowWowFlex home gym.

Top Dog Names of 2010:
 5. Lucy
 4. Bella
 3. Daisy
 2. Max
 1. Buddy

Top Cat Names of 2010:
 5. Smokey
 4. Molly
 3. Bella (pet owners love *Twilight*)
 2. Midnight
 1. Lucy

Pets cause more than 86,000 accidental falls each year. Dogs are the worst culprits, responsible for 7.5 times as many injuries as cats, thanks to their often larger size and daily walks.

SLEEP

Want to stay slim? Go back to bed for a few more hours. Besides making you grumpy and impairing your driving, a lack of sleep may also make you chubby. A number of studies have found a strong link between sleep problems and obesity, including one by the New York Obesity Nutrition Research Center, which found sleep-deprived subjects burn about the same number of calories as those without sleep issues, yet consume about 300 more calories each day. So quit staying up late eating junk food.

᠅

It really is possible to be half asleep. Despite popular belief that the brain is either fully awake or fully asleep, U.S. and Italian researchers believe that neurons in different parts of the brain can shut off for brief periods, even while we are fully awake and active. These neurons are especially likely to go "off line" during long periods without sleep, so if you're feeling like you are not all there, you may be right.

᠅

Women may need more sleep than men. A study of 956 men and women between the ages of 59 and 79 years old found that women slept an average of 16 minutes longer than men. Another study found that on average women have been found to wake up about 30 minutes earlier than men, and their sleep-wake cycle (aka circadian rhythm) is six minutes shorter.

STAIN REMOVAL

Get a barbecue stain on your white t-shirt? You'd be surprised what can remove it. Some strange stain removers you may have lying around the house include:

- Artificial sweeteners: absorbs the oil from grease stains

- Milk: soaking a garment in the stuff overnight removes ink stains

- Toothpaste: also great with ink stains

- Shaving cream: surprisingly good with tomato juice stains

TOOTHPASTE

Brushing your teeth can help your heart. Studies have shown that bad dental hygiene, including bleeding gums and unhealthy teeth, can lead to heart disease. Bacteria can enter an open blood vessel in the mouth and enter the bloodstream, disrupting the flow of blood to the heart and running the risk of a heart attack. Bad breath can do more than just kill your social life.

Terrible dental care and tooth loss was common as recently as World War II, during which the U.S. armed forces had to keep lowering standards in order to get enough recruits. Originally, at least six pairs of opposing teeth were required, but when too few men hit this minimum, standards were lowered to require jaws strong enough to support dentures.

Spearmint and peppermint may be the standard flavors of toothpaste, but some innovators have tried to be a bit more creative:

- Poynter Products rolled out bourbon and scotch flavored toothpastes in 1954, containing 3 percent alcohol.

- Neiman-Marcus manufactured a set of California wine flavored toothpaste. The set of three included Chablis, Burgundy, and Extra-Dry Champagne flavors.

- The Japanese manufacturer Kobayashi Pharmaceuticals decided white and blue pastes were too cliché and rolled out Sumigaki—charcoal toothpaste.

- Unilever Philippines introduced a limited edition chocolate-flavored toothpaste to their Closeup Flavalicious line in 2005.

VACUUMING

Hubert Cecil Booth, the inventor of the first vacuum cleaner to use a power source, demonstrated how his machine would work by placing his mouth on the back of a plush restaurant seat and sucking in. Though he told a newspaper "I almost choked," his experiments led to the "Puffing Billy," a massive oil-powered vacuum cleaner that had to be transported by horse-drawn cart. Most notably, it was used to clean the carpet under the throne in Westminster Abbey in preparation of King Edward VII's coronation.

> The first portable vacuum cleaner, invented in San Francisco in 1905, weighed 92 pounds.

Vacuuming up fleas actually kills them. In tests that used a vacuum cleaner to suction up groups of fleas at all stages of life from a tightly woven carpet, the vacuum proved deadly for 96 percent of adult fleas and all of the pupae and larvae. The researchers repeated the experiment several times before determining that the physical trauma of being sucked into the vacuum was just too much for the little guys.

CHAPTER 9

OUT & ABOUT

Trippy facts about trips out

✈ AIR TRAVEL

The world's first airline transported passengers in blimps. DELAG (short for *Deutsche Luftschiffahrts-Aktiengesellschaft*, or German Airship Transportation Corporation Ltd), founded in 1909, offered scheduled blimp service between Berlin and southern Germany, which took a mere nine hours, compared to 24 hours by rail.

Early flight attendants were all male, and known as "stewards" or "cabin boys." The first female flight attendant was 25-year-old Ellen Church, a registered nurse hired by United Airlines in 1930 to serve as what was then called an "air hostess."

⊨⊰

A Boeing 747 has six million parts, half of which are fasteners.

⊨⊰

Despite what those plague movies might have you thinking, very few people who board a plane with a sick and contagious person will become sick themselves. Researchers have determined there is a two-seat "danger zone" where the flu can actually be transmitted from one passenger to another. If you are any further than two seats beside, in front of, or behind the coughing sneezer, there is little chance you will be infected.

> In the 1930s, before sound systems were installed in airplanes, the cabin crew would use a small megaphone to communicate with passengers.

Boarding planes at random actually goes faster than boarding in groups from back to front. Astrophysicist Jason Steffen studied the speed of various boarding methods and found that going in groups causes bottlenecking as everyone struggles to store their luggage into the overhead bins at the same time. It went faster when it was a free-for-all.

Or even better, follow a special method Steffen developed that he promises is twice as fast as the speediest boarding methods used today:

1. Passengers in window seats on one side of the plane board, in alternating rows (row 1, 3, 5, etc.). Then the other side of the plane does the same.

2. Middle seats board in alternating rows, first on one side, then the other, all odd rows again.

3. Those in the aisle rows do the same.

4. Repeat the whole thing with all the even-numbered rows. Simple, right? Yeah, not really. But efficient!

It may be possible to beat jet lag with food. Jet lag happens when our light-based internal clock gets thrown off, but this can be counteracted by getting our food-based clock on the same time as our destination. This may mean fasting for 16 hours, but you'll be ready for breakfast at the right time when you arrive.

BARBECUING

Marinated steaks are safer than non-marinated ones. Research has shown that coating meats with spice-heavy marinades (whether mint, tarragon, rosemary, or others) reduces the amount of cancer-causing heterocyclic amines (HCAs) created while barbecuing. This is likely due to the antioxidant properties of marinade ingredients like rosmarinic acid, carnosol, and carnosic acid. Sprinkle some spice on that ribeye and *voila!* Health food.

CITY LIVING

Living in big cities may be driving you crazy. Imaging scans of people living in large urban centers show stronger reactions to stress than those who live outside cities.

City living may also make you more self-conscious. Psychologists have found that in urban areas where the number of available partners is very high, superficial appearance takes on a greater importance for finding partners and friends.

The wettest city in the world is Cherrapunji, India, with an average yearly rainfall of 498 inches. In the contiguous United States it is Mobile, Alabama, which gets 67 inches of annual rain fall, and an average of 59 rainy days a year, according to WeatherBill, Inc. Though the Pacific Northwest is often viewed as one of the wettest parts of the country, it does not enter the list until Olympia, Washington, the 24th wettest city.

But that is not to be confused with the sweatiest city in America, a distinction earned by Phoenix, Arizona, followed by Las Vegas and Tallahassee. The least sweaty city, based on levels of heat and humidity, is San Francisco.

The most populace county in the United States is Los Angeles, California, with 9,880,000 residents, according to the 2009 U.S. Census. The least populace is Loving County, Texas, with just 82 residents. It may not be bustling, but Loving has the distinction of being the only county in the 2000 Census with no people below the poverty line.

COMMUTING

Commuters are more stressed than riot police or fighter pilots. Researchers compared the heart rate and blood pressure of people in all three professions and found commuters stuck in traffic were by far the most stressed, likely because of their lack of control compared to the others. Listening to awful drive-time radio DJs may also have played a role.

Seven of the ten most congested stretches of highway in the U.S. are in Los Angeles County.

The traffic on Los Angeles' 110 South was responsible for $277,782,000 worth of wasted fuel for 2010, the highest level in the country.

Though it is responsible for rush hour, work travel only constitutes 16 percent of Americans' travel.

Gas prices may be on the rise, but carpooling has seen a huge drop over the past 25 years, with just 10.7 percent of commuters sharing rides in 2005, compared to 19.7 percent in 1980.

DRIVING

GPS systems have been responsible for at least 300,000 automobile accidents. The insurance company Direct Line found that the use of this tool distracts drivers and leads them to hesitate on busy roads and make illegal or dangerous turns.

If that doesn't scare you: You will soon be able to steer a car with your thoughts. Technology developed in Germany allows a driver to connect with a computer using brain sensors that read mental commands like "right," "left," "accelerate," and "brake."

Now if we could just connect the sensors to the GPS, we could sleep for the entire drive and let the computers do the work.

EATING OUT

Want to eat less at a restaurant? Use a bigger fork. A study in the *Journal of Consumer Research* found that when diners at an Italian restaurant were given small forks, they ate more than when they used larger ones. To really cut back on calories, use a pitchfork.

⚏

Originally, a "restaurant" was a place to go for a "restorative" soup, not for a full meal.

⚏

In 1765, a French seller of these "restorative" soups named Boulanger began selling a dish of sheep's feet with white sauce. The local guild of meat sellers took him to court for breaching the strict divisions between the culinary trades (at the time you had to buy cakes from a baker, roasted meat from a rôtisseur, and so on). Boulanger won, marking the birth of the modern restaurant, in which a range of food and drink could be purchased and paid for on one bill.

⚏

It would not be until 17 years later that the first menu would be introduced—at the Grande Taverne de Londres restaurant in the Rue de Richelieu.

In the 2009 Michelin Guide, Tokyo overtook Paris as the culinary capital of the world, with 11 three-star restaurants to the 10 in the French capital.

ESCALATORS

The first working escalator (then called the "inclined elevator") was installed in 1896 in Coney Island, New York, alongside the Old Iron Pier.

Going up escalators makes you more generous than going down. A series of studies has found that people are more likely to donate to a charity table or offer more of their time to answering questions if they were going up to the next floor rather than heading down. The researchers hypothesize that the upward motion triggers unconscious feelings of altruism and beneficence that influence our actions.

EXERCISE

Though scientists have recommended at least 30 minutes of exercise a day, they have found that half of that can still add years to your life. Of course, about one of those years will have been spent exercising in 15-minute chunks, so it's kind of a wash.

The first treadmill was designed by a pair of doctors at the University of Washington in 1952. It was created to help diagnose heart and lung disease.

In 2009, Double Dutch jump rope became a varsity sport at New York City public schools.

FRESH AIR

If you live in a big city, and you like to go outside, there is a good chance you are breathing in germs from dog poop. Researchers from the University of Colorado found "unexpectedly high" levels of bacteria linked with animal feces in each one of the cities they surveyed, including Detroit, Chicago, Cleveland, and Mayville, Wisconsin. It was Detroit that had the highest level of airborne dog poop.

MOBILE PHONES

Cell phones do not cause cancer. In repeated studies, including a recent European study involving nearly 1,000 participants, no link has been found between the use of mobile phones and brain tumors. Despite what you might be wishing on the person in front of you gabbing on their phone, as far as scientists can tell, cell phones are safe.

But they carry plenty of other health hazards. The average mobile phone carries 18 times more potentially harmful germs than the flush handle in a men's restroom, according to tests conducted by British scientists.

At least 13 percent of cell owners admit to pretending to use their phones in order to avoid interacting with people around them (30 percent for those ages 18 to 29). The rest are actually using their phones to avoid interacting with people around them.

PEOPLE WATCHING

Humans often miss things happening right in front of them. Psychological tests show that humans have surprisingly limited attention capacity, with drivers overlooking road hazards when talking on a cell phone; joggers failing to notice a fight; or volunteers being too focused on a given assignment to notice a person in a gorilla suit walk by. This is interesting, but what does it mean if all I see are people in gorilla suits?

PUBLIC TOILETS

The cleanest public toilets are found in national-chain restaurants. The worst are found in gas stations.

> The first toilet in any row of public stalls is the least frequented and contains the least bacteria.

A major battleground for women's suffrage was the public bathroom. Women were not expected to play a major role in public life, so facilities for them were limited. For example, in 1900 there were 40 toilets for men in London's Leicester Square but just 7 for women. Groups like the Ladies Sanitary Association fought for better treatment, and eventually won. Though judging by the lines outside women's restrooms, more work remains to be done.

PUBLIC TRANSPORTATION

The first subway system in the world was built in London. Boston holds the distinction as first subway system in the United States, opened in 1897 (New York's would open seven years later).

If you want to avoid catching a cold on the subway, ride it every day. Commuters who regularly use public transportation are less likely to catch a respiratory infection than those who just ride it occasionally.

New York City has the highest level of subway ridership of any public transit system in the United States, but that's only the fourth highest in the world:

1. Tokyo   3.160 billion (2009)

2. Moscow   2.392 billion (2009)

3. Seoul   2.048 billion (2009)

4. New York City   1.604 billion (2010)

5. Beijing   1.595 billion (2010)

China is home to the world's longest bus—an 83-foot-long vehicle divided into three segments. While it holds up to 300 passengers, the bus is legally allowed to go up to 51 miles per hour, and only works on routes with very few corners to turn.

A nearly extinct species of public transportation are trailer buses. Sometimes called "camel buses" these are formed by hauling a bus body on a semi-trailer, and were popular in Australia, the Netherlands, and South Africa, but fell out of favor decades ago. Some of the last ones still in use can be found in Havana, Cuba, but these gradually began to be phased out beginning in 2008.

SCHOOL

The first high school in America opened in 1821, in Boston, Massachusetts.

Parents might want to think twice about dragging their teenagers out of bed for the painfully early school day. A raft of research has found that teens function best when sleeping from about 11 pm to 8 am, and that starting the school day later results in positive things like fewer teen car crashes, fewer cases of depression, and a decrease in late arrivals and dropouts.

Tough guys and powerful animals may be the most typical kind of school mascots, but sometimes the student body gets creative::

- Sammy the Banana Slug (University of California, Santa Cruz)

- Scrotie the Scrotum (Rhode Island School of Design)

- The Fighting Pickles (North Carolina School of the Arts)

- The Fighting Okra (Delta State University)

- Super Frog the Horned Frog (Texas Christian University)

The most dangerous school sport for females is cheerleading. A survey by the National Center for Catastrophic Sports Injury Research found that cheerleading was responsible for 65.1 percent of all sports injuries for high school girls. For college females it was responsible for 66.7 percent of injuries.

SHOPPING

Money actually can buy you happiness—if you're spending it on the right things. Researchers have found that spending money on experiences like concerts, family trips, or plays leads to higher levels of satisfaction than buying material goods.

Other ways to wring more satisfaction from your dollars:

- Buy several small treats instead of one big splurge. Pleasure fades whether the purchase was a three-week cruise or a weekend road trip, so quantity often trumps quality when it comes to shopping.

- Pay for something now and enjoy it later.

- Spend a bit on charity or a larger cause, which has been found to result in long-term feelings of satisfaction.

⋈

Men are less likely than women to take up a store employee when they ask, "Can I help you find something?" A study of how consumers make wine-purchase decisions found that while men preferred impersonal sources, like online ratings or wine books, women were more likely to trust a personal suggestion, whether from a friend or family member or someone from a wine store.

> Clothing stores might want to rethink hiring supermodel lookalikes to work at their stores. A study found that shoppers with low self-esteem are less likely to buy an item if they see a good-looking employee or fellow customer wearing it. That may explain why mannequins usually don't have heads.

TRAINS

Nearly seven times as many people die in railroad accidents each year as in airplane accidents.

WALKING

Most of us are familiar with road rage, but in crowded cities there is a new scourge to look out for: Sidewalk Rage. Those suffering what researchers have dubbed "Pedestrian Aggressiveness Syndrome," are identifiable for their muttering, scowling, and bumping into fellow pedestrians, and general indifference to others' need for sidewalk space.

⚏

Flip-flops seem harmless, but they might be messing you up with every step. Doctors advise that the spongy material and weak arch support in most pairs of flip-flops can cause feet to roll inward, leading to potential injury and flat feet. One study found that many flip-flop wearers grip their toes as they take a step, which leads to a shorter stride.

CHAPTER 10
INSECTS

The critters that are creepier than you realized

 ## ANTS

The combined mass of all the ants in the Brazilian Amazon is about four times more than that of all its mammals, birds, reptiles, and amphibians combined.

In at least one species of insects, males are totally unnecessary. The *Mycocepurus smithii* species of ant, discovered in 2005, is made up entirely of female clones of the mother. This leaves the queen to reproduce by turning eggs into larvae without fertilization from sperm.

About 20,000 species of ants live around the globe.

Fire ants may be nasty, venomous critters, but they look out for one another. When the ants of the species *Solenopsis invicta* are threatened with drowning or floods, they lock legs and jaws, forming an airtight raft. Multiplied by hundreds or thousands, the raft becomes a strong defense against floods or heavy rains. Just don't mistake it for a life raft.

BEES

Bees can detect bombs with their tongues. Just like police dogs, bees can be trained to associate the odor of explosives with a food reward. When a bee smells the faintest traces of explosives in the field, it extends its proboscis, expecting food.

Bumblebees keep the temperature of their nests between 28°C and 32°C. When it gets too warm, they cool their larvae by fanning their wings; when it gets too cold, they vibrate their wing muscles, creating heat down through their abdomen. Replacing your air conditioning unit with bumblebee nests not recommended.

> Until the 20th century, bumblebees were called "humblebees" because of the humming sound they made.

Bumblebees are considered one of the smartest insects in the world, doing complex calculations to find the shortest route from one flower to the next.

Urban farmers beware: when bees can't find nectar, they are perfectly happy to settle for high-fructose corn syrup. Beekeepers have reported their bees turning a bright red color after visits to a nearby maraschino cherry factory.

More people die from bee stings in the United States than from snake or spider bites.

BEETLES

While frogs often make a snack out of beetles, one species of the insect flips the food chain. The *Epomis* ground beetle attacks frogs, toads and newts, paralyzing its victims with an incision to their back, then devouring them from the legs up. The meal takes a few hours to complete.

Researchers in Michigan have figured out a way to implant machinery into live beetles, using battery power to direct their movement. The batteries are charged by generators implanted into the insects' flight muscles. These cyborg beetles can be used for everything from search and rescue efforts, to surveillance, to environmental monitoring—and apparently to turn the planet into a real-life 50s B-movie.

BUTTERFLY

The males of many species of butterfly practice "mud-puddling" in which they gather on dung or carrion to obtain nutrients like salt and amino acids. These dung-nutrients are then offered to the female as a nuptial gift during mating. So romantic!

The Japanese *lycaenid* butterfly, *Niphanda fusca,* lays its eggs in the nests of carpenter ants. When the caterpillars hatch, they let off an odor that mimics the scent of the high-ranking male ant caste, so their host feeds them in preference to its actual offspring.

CRICKETS

Chivalry is alive and well in the cricket world. Male crickets have been known to risk their lives to protect their mates, staying exposed while the female finds cover in a burrow. While female and male crickets are equally likely to be eaten when either is attacked alone, females are far more likely to survive when attacked while accompanied by their mate.

But they do have to worry about the guy next to them: cannibalism is rife among crickets, and the slow members of the swarm tend to get devoured first.

"Mormon crickets" are not in fact crickets. They are shield-backed katydids that earned their name from attacking the crops of the Mormon settlers in America during the mid-1800s and the name has stuck ever since.

⊨⊨

Crickets have the biggest testicles of any species. That's proportionally, of course, and specifically the *Platycleis affnis*, or tuberous bush cricket. Its testicles are 14 percent of its body mass. Since the average American man weighs about 190 pounds, that would be the equivalent of a guy having 26.6 pound testicles.

EARWIGS

An earwig's pinchers look scary, but its real weapon is a pair of defensive glands in its abdomen that discharge a chemical spray. The spray shoots in the same direction as the pinchers, making for a brutal one-two punch for any would-be attackers.

EDIBLE INSECTS

Since raising livestock produces a significant amount of methane, ammonia, and carbon dioxide, some scientists think there is a potential environmental gain in eating bugs instead. Insects produce less of these harmful greenhouse gasses per unit of body mass than pigs or cattle, reproduce quickly, and require less nourishment, making them a more efficient source of protein in many parts of the world.

The scientific word for bug-eating is "entomophagy."

Spiders are reputed to taste like peanut butter.

FLIES

Flies taste with their feet, allowing them to move quickly from one place to another, sampling as they go and avoiding the fly swatter.

Some flies really can be greedy. Male fruit flies will double the length of time they take to mate with a female when they sense another male nearby. Scientists call this behavior "paranoid", since in these types of flies, the females mate only once, making it unlikely there would be any actual competition. Barry White calls this behavior, "Can't Get Enough of Your Love, Babe."

LICE

Six to twelve million infestations of head lice occur in the U.S. each year.

⚏

Lice are tougher than ever. While simple over-the-counter products may have gotten rid of head lice in the past, the American Academy of Pediatrics is now urging parents to use stronger pesticidal creams, and to apply them more often to fully eradicate the resilient pests.

MOSQUITOS

One mosquito leg can support 23 times the insect's body weight while they walk on water. Their legs are covered with tiny grooves containing pockets of air that keep them afloat thanks to the water's surface tension.

⚏

But unlike other water-walking insects, mosquitos can also walk on walls, thanks to special footpads similar to those possessed by flies. It is truly a wondrous pest.

⚏

Mosquitos are more attracted to people with Type O blood than those with Type A or B. A 2004 study in Japan found that female mosquitos are twice as likely to land on Type O's than Type A's.

Or perhaps the Type O people were just drunk. A study in West Africa found that female mosquitos were attracted to the smell of subjects who had downed a liter of beer over those who had not by a ratio of two to one. So pick up some mosquito repellant along with that 12-pack.

SNAILS

You would think being swallowed and digested by a bird would be enough to kill an insect. Not so for the *Tornatellides boeningi* species of snail, which frequently survives being eaten, digested, and pooped out by its predator, the Japanese white-eyed bird. Studies conducted by researchers from Tohoku University in Japan found that 15 percent of the snails came out the other end alive, though probably in a very bad mood.

SPIDERS

With the exception of one family (*Uloboridae*), all spiders are venomous.

The toughest biological material in the world is likely the silk from the Darwin bark spider, which inhabits tropical areas like Madagascar. Able to absorb serious impact from bees and dragon flies, the silk possesses 10 times the strength of Kevlar, the material used in bulletproof vests.

᛭

The black widow spider is kind of a hog. When the spider gets around a lot of food, it becomes wasteful and a bit lazy, killing food it doesn't need and leaving much of it uneaten.

᛭

While some might call this gluttonous, scientists believe this is a way for the female black widows to attract the males. After enjoying a delicious meal and a satisfying mating session, the female then devours the male. Probably not the first date he had imagined.

STINGS

The bullet ant inflicts the most painful sting in the world. The throbbing, burning waves of pain from its paralyzing venom last for longer than 24 hours.

᛭

The Satere-Mawe people of Brazil use the stings of the bullet ants in warrior initiation rituals. The young men must wear a glove filled with the nasty insects for 10 minutes, usually causing temporary paralysis in their hands and uncontrollable shaking for days. After that, it takes a lot to scare them.

The Schmidt Sting Index scores the relative pain caused by different insect stings on a scale of 0 (benign) to 4 (excruciating). Entomologist Justin Schmidt determined the scores after subjecting himself to the stings of 78 different insects. His rankings and vivid descriptions read like a perverse wine guide:

1.0—Sweat Bee: Light, ephemeral, almost fruity. As if a tiny spark has singed a single hair on your arm.

2.0—Yellow jacket: Hot and smoky, almost irreverent. Imagine W. C. Fields extinguishing a cigar on your tongue.

3.0—Paper Wasp: Caustic burning. Distinctly bitter aftertaste. Like spilling a beaker of hydrochloric acid on a paper cut.

4.0—Bullet Ant: Pure, intense, brilliant pain. Like firewalking over flaming charcoal with a 3-inch rusty nail in your heel.

TERMITES

The termite queen holds the distinction of being the longest-living insect. It is known to live as long as 50 years, and some scientists put it at closer to 100 years.

But she does not live a relaxing life. Termite queens lay as many as 40,000 eggs per day.

WASPS

Wasps are better than bloodhounds at detecting odors. The insects are capable of detecting explosives, drugs, and virtually any other scent they are trained to respond to. Perhaps most exciting to many city-dwellers: they can even detect bedbugs. As the saying goes, it takes a creepy insect to know a creepy insect.

⬛

A species of Costa Rican wasps may win the prize for "Nastiest Parasite on the Planet." The wasp attacks its host, the orb spider, known as *Plesiometa argyra*, temporarily paralyzing it and laying its eggs on the spider's abdomen. The spider regains consciousness and goes about its day of web building as if nothing happened. About two weeks after the attack, the larvae that are growing on the spider's belly, feeding on its juices, compel their host to build a bizarre web—stouter and smaller than its usual. They then burst forth from the spider, killing it, and use the creepy web it built for them as a makeshift wasp's nest. Mother Nature can be really twisted when she wants to be.

WINGS

> Insects flap their wings differently than birds. Since an insect's wings are directly attached to its exoskeleton, it moves its wings by vibrating its whole body.

 ## WORMS

Worms eat about half their weight each day.

The nervous system of a roundworm works just like the human brain, only simpler. Scientists use the millimeter-long insect to understand how neurons and synapses and other brain connections function, and the information can be extrapolated to the same functions of the human brain.

CHAPTER 11

ANIMALS

Furry, scaly, feathered, and strange

ALLIGATORS

During warm seasons, alligators often leave their swamps and seek out sun and watering holes in swimming pools, city streets, and on front porches. In alligator-rich areas like Florida, it's not uncommon for them to slip into homes through open doggy doors or garages.

ARMADILLOS

Armadillos are the only animals other than humans that can contract leprosy. About a third of leprosy cases in the U.S. occur as a result of contact with the armored critters, particularly in Louisiana and Texas, where eating armadillos is not uncommon.

BABIES

For a number of animals, including crocodiles, turtles, and some birds, sex is not determined genetically, but by the temperature of the eggs. Cooler temperatures result in males, warmer temperatures lead to females.

BABOONS

For baboons at least, it pays to be a nice guy. While the alpha male may enjoy a more prominent position and more mates than he knows what to do with, research finds that being a "beta male" means lower stress and plenty of mating opportunities. Just without all the fights over territory and female baboons.

BATS

The bat is the only mammal that can fly.

One creature's deathtrap is another's favorite nap spot. A species of vesper bat gets its rest during the day by squeezing into the throat of the carnivorous pitcher plant. Folding up its wings, the bat finds a resting place safely above the pool of digestive fluid at the bottom of the leaf where small insects typically meet their end. But the bat is no freeloader: in exchange for the leafy hammock, the bat releases nitrogen, which is valuable for the pitcher plant's health.

BEARS

Polar bears are moving to land. A 20-year study by the U.S. Geological Survey found that the proportion of polar bears that make dens on ice dropped from 62 percent in 1985 to 37 percent in 2005.

> The change in habitat is also leading the polar bears to mate with brown bears again, something that scientists believe has not happened since the last ice age. Though the researchers have yet to agree whether they should be called "grolar bears" or "pizzlies."

The sun bear may be the smallest member of the bear family, but it has the longest tongue. Measuring as long as 10 inches, the slender tongue is perfect for hunting honey in bee hives in tree trunks.

⊨⊧

Sloth bears have impressive olfactory skills, and are able to detect grubs as deep as three feet below the ground's surface. When it discovers an anthill, the sloth sucks up the ants through its muzzle, creating a hovering sound that can be heard nearly 600 feet away.

BIRDS

City birds have bigger brains than country birds. European researchers compared the brain sizes of 82 species of birds and found that the "urban adapters" have significantly larger brains relative to their body size than those in more rural areas. More brains to better target more people with bird-doo bombs, no doubt.

⊨⊧

The Nazca booby may have a silly name, but these Galapagos Islands seabirds can be nasty. When two siblings are born, the oldest shoves the youngest out of the nest, leaving it to be gobbled by a predator or die of thirst. This siblicide is attributed partly to high levels of testosterone in the hatchlings. Those that survive bullying turn into bullies themselves as they get older, repeating the cycle of violence and abuse.

Speaking of angry birds, the Kea, a species of New Zealand parrot, usually eats roots, insects, and carrion, but has been known to go after sheep, dogs, and even horses. It uses its curved beak to cut into the animal and eat the fat from it—the animals then dies from blood poisoning or by accident while trying to escape. Though it doesn't prey on humans, the Kea aggressively seeks out scraps, even tearing at boots, backpacks, and cars.

CHICKENS

Chickens see color better than humans. While human retinas are only sensitive to red, blue, and green wavelengths, chickens also have cones that detect violet wavelengths and a "double cone" that helps them detect motion.

CHIMPANZEES

Chimps eat dirt. Scientists believe they do this because it prevents malaria when combined with certain plants, like the *Trichilia rubescens*.

Overturning expectations, bonobos beat chimpanzees in a series of intelligence tests conducted by the Royal Zoological Society of Antwerp in 2011. While chimps were believed to be the smarter creatures, they were too busy fighting for dominance to solve the puzzles.

CROCODILES

"Crocodile tears" is more than just an expression. Crocodiles cry when they eat. The glands that keep their eyes moist are near their throats, so they tear up as they swallow.

> A crocodile can shift its internal organs backwards in its body, should an emergency arise.

Once under water, a crocodile can slow its heart rate to two or three beats per minute, going up to an hour without breathing.

DEER

Deer are deadly. Over the five years from 2005 through 2009, vehicle-animal collisions led to the deaths of 1,017 people, three quarters of them because of deer, according to the Insurance Institute for Highway Safety. At an average of 203 deaths per year, deer cause more deaths than airplane crashes (responsible for just 138 deaths per year).

DOLPHINS

Dolphin skin is kind of miraculous. It heals far more quickly than most animal skin, resisting infection by using stem cells to rebuild missing or damaged tissues from injuries (particularly shark bites). It can regenerate large chunks of blubber with no scarring or signs of deformity.

ELEPHANTS

The elephant's gestation period is the longest of any land animal—a whopping 22 months.

Elephants actually don't forget. Researchers have witnessed parents recognizing their offspring after decades of separation. In a separate study, the creatures reacted with fear when they detected the scent of garments worn by men of a tribe known to spear elephants to prove their virility. They only reacted mildly to the scent of garments worn by a different, less hostile, tribe.

FISH

Goldfish get paler if kept in a dark room. Their chromatophore cells do not produce as much pigment in the dark, so their colors naturally fade.

The most venomous fish in the world is the stonefish. The greenish-brown creature is not much to look at, but anyone who steps on the poisonous spines along its back will suffer excruciating pain and, without treatment, could die.

FLAMINGOS

Flamingos only eat with their heads upside down.

The birds also use erectile tissue to help them swallow. The tissue, on the floor of the flamingo's mouth, fills with blood, which stabilizes its mouth and tongue and makes it easier for it to do its odd upside-down eating.

FROGS

Frogs shut their eyes when they shoot their tongue out to catch prey. They also keep them shut while eating, since their eyes help them to swallow—their eyeballs sinking through openings in the skull to help force food down their throat.

GROUPS

Whole books have been written on the bizarre collective nouns we've come up with for animals, but here are a few favorites:

* A ballet of swans   * A business of ferrets

* A charm of falcons

* A generation of vipers

* A mask of raccoons

* A squabble of seagulls

* A drift of swine

* An intrigue of kittens

* An ostentation of peacocks

* A wisdom of owls

A group of geese on the ground is a gaggle; when it takes to the sky, it becomes a skein.

HARES

Hares box one another during spring mating season. While many believed this was the males fighting among each other for a female, it turns out it was the females swiping at the males to block their advances.

JELLYFISH

All jellyfish sting their prey, but only a few species can cause a reaction in humans. Some species, like the notorious *Irukandji* jellyfish, can kill. While most jellyfish have stingers on their tentacles, puncturing the victim's flesh with millions of microscopic pricks, the *Irukandji* also has stingers on its body. It is believed to be the most venomous creature in the world.

The largest jellyfish species in the world is the lion's mane jellyfish. The largest recorded specimen, which washed up on the shore of Massachusetts Bay in 1870, had a body with diameter of 7 feet 6 inches, and tentacles measuring 120 feet long.

⊨⊰

Most jellyfish do not have brains. They use a network of nervous systems called a "nerve net." The net can detect other animals or objects and send the message throughout a circular nerve ring on the rim of the jellyfish body.

⊨⊰

The typical jellyfish lifespan ranges from a few hours to a few months, though one species is reported to live as long as 30 years. The species *Turritopsis nutricula* is able to transform from the fully developed "medusa" back into the germinal "polyp" over and over again, effectively becoming immortal.

LIONS

What lions boast in speed, they lack in stamina. A lionesses' heart makes up just 0.57 percent of her body weight (a hyena's is close to 1 percent, while a greyhound's can be as large as 1.73 percent). That's why they run in short bursts, usually trying to get close to prey before attacking.

⊨⊰

When a younger, fitter male lion overthrows the older leader of the pride, he often kills off all the cubs that are not his own to ensure future offspring will have his genes.

A lion can eat about 40 pounds of meat in one sitting.

MICE

Scientists in Texas have found a way to create a baby mouse from two male mice. They clone a mother mouse from a male, which then mates with another male, producing offspring carrying the genes of the two guys. They hope this will help with repopulation efforts for endangered species—or help create a breed of super-manly mice.

OSTRICH

Despite popular belief, ostriches do not bury their heads in the sand. This misconception may have originated because the birds frequently graze on small stones to help with digestion, or because they sleep with their heads on the ground, which could look like it's buried from a distance away. But despite how useful it may be as a political metaphor, the ostrich does not stick its head in the sand when threatened—it runs really fast in the other direction.

PARROTS

Among the animals that have been found to possess the ability to reason are humans, chimps, and most recently . . . the African Grey Parrot. In studies, researchers showed the parrot three cups, with a seed in one of them and a walnut under another. They shuffled the cups behind a screen, removing either the seed or the walnut. When they showed the parrot which of the treats had been removed, the bird was able to piece together which cup still held some food.

PENGUINS

Penguins can remain underwater for up to 20 minutes. This is made possible by cutting off oxygen to their muscles and letting oxygenation of the heart and brain take priority.

PIGS

Nearly half of the world's pigs are kept by farmers in China.

RATS

It is possible to turn the memories of rats on and off with a switch. When signals between two parts of the rat's brain are interrupted, it immediately forgets how to do a task it has learned: pressing a lever in order to get a reward. When the signals resume, the rat remembers again.

Love can be deadly. That is certainly the case for rats infected with the parasite *Toxoplasma gondii*. The parasite can only reproduce in cats, so when it infects a rat, it tweaks its usual instincts, causing the smell of cat urine to charge up the neurons that would normally be triggered by another rat. The love-struck vermin seeks out the source of this arousing smell only to end up as Fluffy's dinner and provide the *T. gondii* with a lovely new host in which to reproduce.

SNAKES

Rattlesnake mating sessions can last more than 22 hours.

SQUID

Squid sex is romantic. And by romantic, I mean totally revolting. When a male squid wants to get down, it cuts a two-inch deep wound into the female into which it then inserts its sperm. The sperm then burrows deeper into the female by dissolving her tissue and is then fertilized. The miracle of life.

A group of British biologists believes it's time the ocean had its own mascot, and that the mascot should be a giant squid, similar to how the panda has become the symbol of the World Wildlife Fund. They have a number of reasons for the selection, such as how the species reflects concerns about overfishing, pollution, and climate change—but the biggest reason is that people are just really into giant squids.

SUICIDE

Accidental mass suicide is not uncommon in the animal world. In Manitoba, Canada, in 1985, and then again in 2003, flocks of dead geese were found with injuries indicating that they had flown directly into the ground. Researchers believe it was related to weather disturbances which might have disoriented the flock.

> In November 2010, on their way to the local market, 52 sheep in Turkey leapt off a cliff. But while their herder was distraught, he could take comfort in the fact that things could have been worse: five years earlier, 1,500 sheep jumped off a cliff in Turkey, although most of them survived.

WALRUSES

The male walrus is equipped with a penis bone (called a baculum) that extends up to 30 inches long, the longest of any living mammal.

WHALES

Whales are one of very few mammals that experience menopause. Elephants, chimpanzees, rhesus monkeys, and humans are the others.

CHAPTER 12

NATURE

Our bizarre, beautiful world

AIR

Air pollution may contribute to ear infections. Children in areas with lower air quality are about 10 percent more likely to suffer from infection than those in areas where air quality is higher.

CLOUDS

A cloud is classified into one of 10 categories based on its appearance and height. These categories were actually determined and agreed upon at the Cloud Committee of the International Meteorological Conference in 1896 and published as the *International Cloud Atlas*.

The highest clouds in the sky are noctilucent, or "night shining," clouds, with ragged edges and often too faint to be seen.

DIAMONDS

Diamonds can patch up more than a lovers' spat. Scientists have found that injecting "nanodiamonds"—clusters of tiny carbon atoms—into someone receiving chemotherapy treatment may help protect the healthy white blood cells from being poisoned along with the cancerous ones. A study on mice found there were no toxic effects on the creatures when injected with the diamonds.

> If you leave a diamond in the sun it gets smaller. Sure, it happens extremely slowly, but Australian physicists have found that applying UV rays to a diamond causes it to lose atoms, smoothing rough edges or creating small pits in the diamond surface. So remember to keep your tiaras inside on sunny days.

EARTH

The Earth is not actually round. Well, not perfectly round: its girth is about 0.3 percent greater than its height.

⚏

If you separated the Earth into its component materials, it would break down roughly as:

32.1%	Iron
30.1%	Oxygen
15.1%	Silicon
13.9%	Magnesium

⚏

Earth does not actually take 24 hours to rotate on its axis. The actual time is closer to 23 hours, 56 minutes, and four seconds (scientists call this a "sidereal day"). Similarly, a year is precisely 365.2564 days long. The additional day in a leap year lets us catch up every four years, with an extra 0.0256 days to spare.

FLOWERS

Air pollution destroys the smell of flowers. While scent molecules of flowers growing in natural areas can travel as far as 4,000 feet, in polluted areas downwind of major cities, they can only travel between 650 and 980 feet.

The "corpse flower" plays by different rules than most floral species. As its name implies, the massive flower, which only blossoms for a few hours before laying dormant for years, lets out the smell of decaying flesh to attract scavenging beetles that feed on the stuff. Though the insects find no carcass, they leave the flower covered in its pollen, which they carry to the next corpse flower, pollinating it and helping it propagate the species.

FUNGI

A half-ton, 33-foot-long fungus was discovered in China in 2011. The largest ever discovered at the time, the massive "fungal fruiting body," similar to a mushroom, got so big by feeding on rotting wood.

GOLD

Gold is the planet's 73rd most abundant element. The only elements more rare (and more expensive) are:

* Iridium   * Platinum

* Osmium   * Rhodium

⊨⊰

While it may be heavy, gold is extremely soft. An ounce of the stuff can be stretched into a wire 50 miles long, or flattened into a (very thin) sheet with an area of 100 square feet.

⊨⊰

About 70 percent of the world's gold output is used for jewelry, according to the World Gold Council. Just 13 percent is used for coins, bought by investors, or put into central banks.

LAKES

The longest name of any place in the United States is the 45-letter *Chargoggagoggmanchauggagoggchaubunagungamaugg*, a lake in Webster, Massachusetts. It is Algonquin for, "Fishing Place at the Boundaries—Neutral Meeting Grounds," or as a local newspaper editor translated, "You fish on your side, I fish on my side, and nobody fish in the middle."

With little warning lakes can turn blood red. No, this is not a sign of the apocalypse, but due to naturally occurring bacteria called *Chromatiaceae* that thrive in oxygen-deprived water. But while they may not signify End Times, red lakes are generally not too hospitable to the fish and other creatures that need oxygen to survive.

MOON

The moon is shrinking. Spotting cracks on the moon's surface, scientists determined that faults were formed as the moon's core cooled and shrank over the eons. From what they could determine, it has shrunk about 200 yards over the millions of years, out of a diameter of 2,160 miles. As shrinkage goes, that's nothing to be embarrassed about.

Gravity on the Moon is about 1/6 the strength of the Earth's gravity. So a 150 pound person weighs just 25 pounds on the moon.

MOUNTAINS

Glaciers are holding mountains down. Radar images of the Earth's surface demonstrate that glaciers are wearing away at mountaintops and over the centuries have been more responsible for the height difference of the planet's mountain ranges than tectonic shifts, which scientists usually credit for the size difference.

The tallest mountain on Earth is not Mt. Everest. While it towers 8,850 meters high, the winner should actually be Hawaiian volcano Mauna Kea, which may only stand 4,205 meters *above* sea level, but from base to highest tip registers at an impressive 10,314 meters in height.

OCEANS

Rip tides kill more people each year than sharks, jellyfish or massive waves combined.

A new sea is growing in the middle of Africa. Scientists expect that a 35-mile rift in the Ethiopian dessert Afar, which opened up in 2005, will eventually create a new sea, at a rate of less than an inch per year. Eventually the Red Sea is expected to pour into the new sea over a period of about a million years. So hold off on buying that globe.

The sperm whale is one of the deepest divers in the ocean, capable of dipping 6,500 feet below the surface (more than five times the height of the Empire State Building).

PLANETS

Neptune takes 164 years to orbit the Sun, making it the laziest planet since Pluto was stripped of its planethood in 2006 (it took 248 years for a full orbit).

Pluto was named by an 11-year-old girl. In 1930, Venetia Phair suggested the name to her grandfather, a friend of one of the astronomers responsible for giving it a name. Despite popular belief, the name came from the god of the underworld, not the Disney dog.

PLANTS

Plants produce their own painkillers. When stressed by drought, cold, or insect infestation, plants emit a chemical called methyl salicylate—a form of aspirin.

Mustard plants serve as chemical telephones between insects above and below ground. Since some root-eating insects prefer not to eat a plant that's being munched by a leaf-eating insect, it will send a chemical signal up through a plant's roots into its leaves. When the leaf-eater starts to feast it quickly gets the root-eater's message and moves along to an unoccupied plant.

SPACE

Bad news for future colonists of Mars: humans can't procreate in outer space. Ionizing radiation throughout the solar system reduces male sperm count and sterilizes female eggs. For those who would be able to conceive, their baby would have a higher chance of suffering birth defects, or at least sterilization (though scientists are working on space-shield technology to protect humans from this radiation).

> Space smells like a NASCAR race. Because of by-products given off during the combustion of dying stars, space is pervaded by a burning odor similar to hot metal, diesel fumes, and barbecue.

STARS

There are between 200 and 400 billion stars in our galaxy.

But there may be many more than that, according to some astronomers who used the powerful scientific instruments at the W.M. Keck Observatory in Hawaii. They were able to detect the faint images of red dwarf stars in what scientists call "elliptical galaxies" located between about 50 million and 300 million light-years away. This would triple the total number of known stars in the universe.

SUN

The sun is big. Like, really big. Specifically, it makes up 99.87% of our solar system's mass. It's also approximately 333,000 times the size of Earth.

⋈

The sun's atmosphere is hotter than its surface. Scientists believe this is due to plasma fountains called spicules, which constantly shoot up from the surface at about 186,000 miles per hour.

TEMPERATURE

The hottest inhabited place on the planet is Dallol, Ethiopia. Its average annual temperature sits at 93 degrees Fahrenheit.

⋈

The record for hottest temperature recorded on Earth stands at 3.6 billion degrees Fahrenheit, or 2 billion degrees Kelvin. It was produced in a lab by superheated gas at Sandia National Laboratories. By comparison: the interior of the Sun is a measly 15 million degrees Kelvin.

TREES

The tallest tree in the world is a California redwood, standing 379 feet (slightly taller than the length of a football field).

＊

The highest trees have been found to grow is between 400 and 426 feet high. This height limit is the result of two forces at work: the upward growth that pushes the tree up, toward stronger sunlight, and the downward force of gravity, which makes it tough to push water all the way from the roots to its highest branches.

＊

You probably know that you can determine a tree's age by its number of rings, but the reason for this is that it forms new, light-colored wood in the spring and summer. During the fall and winter, any new cells are usually smaller and have darker thick walls, so the wood is darker as well, creating an annual ring.

＊

Tree rings get wider during wet, good-growing years, so everything from ancient droughts to hurricane activity can be detected by looking at the rings.

WATER

You can die from drinking too much water. Officially known as "water intoxication," this overhydration is especially likely to occur in those participating in activities that promote heavy sweating, as they drink large amounts of water to replace their lost fluid. The 2002 Boston Marathon competitor Cynthia Lucero, and Washington D.C. police officer James McBide are two recent cases of lethal overhydration.

⊨⊰

Hot water freezes faster than cold water. This is due to a combination of scientific factors summarily called, "the Mpemba effect," named after the Tanzanian student who noticed the phenomenon during a class project. Aristotle, Francis Bacon and René Descartes have also noted this surprising fact.

⊨⊰

When the United States government began putting fluoride into drinking water in the 1950s and 1960s, some believed it was a Communist plot to undermine national health.

The same water that existed on the earth millions of years ago is still present today. Because of the earth's closed cycle of evaporation, condensation, and precipitation, that glass of water you just drank was at one time dinosaur pee.

Ice is big business. As of 2002, there were 426 commercial ice-making companies in the United States, with a value of nearly $600 million.

WEEDS

The French word for dandelion, *pissenlit*, means "piss the bed." It's called this because of the dandelion leaves' diuretic properties.

⋈

Many backyard weeds could serve as ingredients for a very healthy salad. Dandelions are packed with vitamins A, C and K, as well as calcium, iron, manganese, and potassium. Velvety Lamb's-quarters are healthier than spinach, with 10 times the recommended daily dose of vitamin K. Stinging nettles can make a delicious and healthy tea (just be sure you handle them properly or you will find them quite injurious to your well-being). .

THE END

The end of the world has been predicted to occur on specific dates dozens of times. Some notable predictions:

- 1658: Christopher Columbus stated that the world was created in 5343 BC, and would last 7000 years.

- 1697, then 1716, then 1736: The Puritan minister Cotton Mather revised his prediction of the End Times twice. He died in 1728, sure that third time was the charm.

- July, 1999: The ever-vague Nostradamus's predictions that a "King of Terror" would come from the sky in "1999 and seven months" had people who pay attention to Nostradamus's predictions very nervous.

- 2000: Isaac Newton, in his book Observations upon the Prophecies of Daniel, and the Apocalypse of St. John, predicted Christ would return at the start of the new millennium.

SOURCES

CHAPTER 1—FOOD & DRINK

Apple Pie: Hendrickson, Paul. "Savoring Pie Town." *Smithsonian* Feb. 2005.

Schmidt, Stephen. "Apple Pie: A Slice of America's Past." *The Washington Post*, 25 Sept. 1991.

Shaw, Mary-Liz. "The Apple Pie Lie." *The Pantagraph*. 28 Oct. 2009.

Apples: Yepsen, Roger. *Apples*. New York: W.W. Norton & Company, Inc., 1994.

"EWG's 2011 Shopper's Guide to Pesticides in Produce." Environmental Working Group. June 2011.

Bananas: Castle, Matt. "The Unfortunate Sex Life of the Banana." *Damn Interesting* blog, 24 Aug. 2009.

Barclay, Eliza. "Slippery Banana Peels Could Be A Savior For Polluted Water." *NPR Shots* blog, 11 Aug. 2011.

Beer: Adams, Cecil. "Are brown bottles better for beer?" *The Straight Dope* blog, 28 Jan. 2011.

Chocolate: Buitrago-Lopez, Adriana. "Chocolate consumption and cardiometabolic disorders: systematic review and meta-analysis." *British Medical Journal.* 29 Aug. 2011.

The American Heritage Dictionary.

"Chocolate 'better than kissing.'" *BBC News*. 16 Apr. 2007.

Coffee: De Koning Gans, J. Margot, et al. "Tea and Coffee Consumption and Cardiovascular Morbidity and Mortality." *Arteriosclerosis, Thrombosis, and Vascular Biology*. 18 June 2010.

Cookies: Brunner, Borgna. "The History of the Fortune Cookie." *Information Please Database*. Pearson Education, Inc. 2007.

Olson, Mike. "Which Girl Scout Cookies Score the Most Brownie Points?" *Wired*. 30 Aug. 2011.

Cupcakes: "Cake History." *The Food Timeline*. Web. Accessed: 12 Oct. 2011.

http://www.neimanmarcus.com

Doughnuts: *Online Etymology Dictionary*.

"'Old Salt' Doughnut Hole Inventor Tells Just How Discovery Was Made and Stomach of Earths Saved." *The Washington Post*. 25 Mar. 1916.

Energy Drinks: Arria, Amelia, et al. "Energy drink consumption and increased risk for alcohol dependence." *Alcoholism: Clinical & Experimental Research*. Feb. 2011.

Sampson, Zinie Chen. "Now that's a buzz: Alcohol-laced energy drinks turned into ethanol." *Fuelfix* blog. 6 Jan. 2011.

Seifert, Sara M., et al. "Health Effects of Energy Drinks on Children, Adolescents, and Young Adults." *Pediatrics*. Web. 14 Feb. 2011.

Fast Food: Ver Ploeg, Michele, et al. "Access to Affordable and Nutritious Food—Measuring and Understanding Food Deserts and Their Consequences: Report to Congress." United States Department of Agriculture Report to Congress. June 2009.

Zhong, Chen-Bo, and Sanford DeVoe, "You Are How You Eat: Fast Food and Impatience," *Psychological Science*, 2010.

Fatty Foods: DiPatrizio, Nicholas, et al. "An endocannabinoid signal in the gut controls dietary fat intake." *PNAS*. 4 July 2011.

Fish: Stiles, Margot, et al. "Bait and Switch: How Seafood Fraud Hurts Our Oceans, Our Wallets and Our Health." *Oceana*. 2011.

Christen, William, et al. "Dietary Omega-3 Fatty Acid and Fish Intake and Incident Age-Related Macular Degeneration in Women." *Archives of Ophthalmology*. Web. 14 Mar. 2011.

Garlic: "Does garlic protect against vampires? An experimental study." *Discover Magazine's Discoblog.* 18 Aug. 2009.

Hamburgers: Ozersky, Josh. "The Story of the Hamburger, Part One: The Past." *Eater.* 26 April 2011.

Cobe, Patricia. "Not the same old grind: beef is still our top burger choice, but variations on the all-American patty are gaining ground." *Restaurant Business.* 15 Jan. 2004.

Honey: American Bear Association. www.americanbear.org.

Neff, Kelly Joyce. "The healing power of honey: From burns to weak bones, raw honey can help." *Natural News.* 26 Jan. 2007.

Adams, Stephen. "Tea tree honey 'could fight MRSA.'" *The Telegraph.* 13 Apr. 2011.

Ice: O'Connor, Anahad. "The Claim: A Craving for Ice Is a Sign of Anemia." *The New York Times.* 21 June 2010.

Ketchup: Rawsthorn, Alice. "An Icon, Despite Itself." *The New York Times.* 12 Apr. 2009.

Kerrigan, Lynn. "No Matter How You Spell It, America's Favorite Condiment," *The Global Gourmet.* Web. July 1999.

Buie, Elizabeth. "Sauce splodger seeks similar." *The Herald.* 5 May 1998.

Pruess, Joanna. "Squeezed Out of Our Cupboards; ketchups Worth Keeping." *The Washington Post.* 29 Sept. 1993.

Lunch: Ronca, Debra. "The History of the Lunch Box." *TLC Cooking.* Web. Accessed: 12 Nov. 2011.

Raloff, Janet. "Bag lunches invite disease, study finds." *Science News.* 9 Aug. 2011.

Meat: Weise, Elizabeth. "CDC: Over 50? Heat cold cuts to 165 degrees to avoid listeria." *USA Today.* 4 May 2011.

Melons: "Investigation Announcement: Multistate Outbreak of Listeriosis Linked to Rocky Ford Cantaloupes." Center for Disease Control. 12 Sept. 2011.

Milk: Boyle, Rebecca. "Genetically Modified Cows Produce Milk Akin To Human Milk." *PopSci.* 4 Apr. 2011.

McCane, Widdowson, et al. "Milk Composition Analysis." International Laboratory Services. Web. Accessed: 13 Nov. 2011.

Mustard: Zamarra, Galen. "The Proper Mustard," *Art Culinaire*. 22 June 2007.

Dobbin, Ben. "French's mustard, tangy sensation of 1904 World's Fair, still fills an insatiable demand." *Associated Press*. 4 July 2004.

Pork: USDA Census of Agriculture, 1997. Web. Accessed: 14 Nov. 2011.

Potato Chips: "Joe 'Spud' Murphy." *The Telegraph*. 5 Nov. 2001.

Mozaffarian, Dariush, et al. "Changes in Diet and Lifestyle and Long-Term Weight Gain in Women and Men." *New England Journal of Medicine*. 23 June 2011.

Poultry: Batz, Michael, et al. "Ranking the Risks: The 10 Pathogen-Food Combinations With The Greatest Burden on Public Health." *University of Florida Emerging Pathogens Institute*. 28 Apr. 2011.

Salt: Bernstein, Adam M., and Walter C. Willett. "Trends in 24-h urinary sodium excretion in the United States, 1957-2003; a systematic review." *American Journal of Clinical Nutrition*. Nov. 2010.

Kurlansky. Mark. *Salt: A World History*. New York: Bloomsbury Publishing, 2002.

Brewer's Dictionary of Phrase and Fable.

Norris, Dayna. "Salt: The Only Rock We Eat." *The Iowa Source*. Oct. 2004.

Sandwiches: Carlos, Brenda. "Fascinating Facts About Sandwiches." *Chefs.com*. Web. Accessed: 12 Oct. 2011.

Spicy Food: Gorman, James. "A Perk of Our Evolution: Pleasure in Pain of Chilies." *The New York Times*. 20 Sept. 2010.

Morrow, Jean. "Buffalo Wings." *AOL Slash/Food*. 27 July 2007.

Karp, David. "Market Watch: Super-hot Bhut Jolokia chiles." *Los Angeles Times*. 7 Jan. 2011.

"Spice Fights Colon Cancer." *Ivanhoe Newswire*. 3 Aug. 2006.

Sugar: Dickinson, Rachel. "How Sugar Coated the World." *Christian Science Monitor*. Aug. 2003.

Babowice, Hope. "Sugar has been a sweet treat for hundreds of years." *Daily Herald*. 12 Dec. 1996.

"Sugar Facts." American Sugar Alliance. Web. Accessed: 27 Oct. 2011.

Veggies: "Eating greens 'best way to look good', research shows." *BBC*. 13 Jan. 2011.

Whisky: Donnelly, Brian. "Toast to a whisky 70 years in the making." *Herald Scotland*. 11 Mar. 2010.

CHAPTER 2—LOVE & SEX

Arousal: Alexander, Brian. "No girls allowed? Sometimes, testosterone zone makes sense." MSNBC.com. Web. 9 Aug. 2011.

"Saffron and ginseng 'shown to boost sexual desire.'" *The Telegraph*. 28 Mar. 2011.

Attraction: "Happy Guys Finish Last, Says New Study On Sexual Attractiveness." *ScienceDaily*. 26 May 2011.

Baumeister, Roy, and JP Mendoza. "Cultural Variations in the Sexual Marketplace: Gender Equality Correlates with More Sexual Activity." *Journal of Social Psychology*. May-June 2011.

"The Global Gender Gap Report." World Economic Forum. 2006.

Bachelors: "From Carver to Beatty, Famous Bachelors." *Albany Times Union*. 15 Sept. 1990.

Beauty: Briggs, Helen. "Beauty sleep concept is not a myth, says study." *BBC News*. 14 Dec. 2010.

"2010 Plastic Surgery Procedural Statistics." American Society of Plastic Surgeons. Web. Accessed: 11 Oct. 2011.

Birth Control: Brooks, Helen. "Briefing: A rival to the pill." *The Times*. 10 May 2009.

Break Ups: McCandless, David. "The beauty of data visualization." TED.com. Web. Accessed: 11 Dec. 2011.

"Heartbreak Puts the Brakes On Your Heart." *ScienceDaily*. 29 Sept. 2010.

Breasts: Goldwert, Lindsay. "Bra company debuts L cup; Women's lingerie sizes getting large, average U.S. size is 38D." *New York Daily News*. 21 Jan. 2011.

Schnurnberger, Lynn. *Let There Be Clothes: 40,000 Years of Fashion*. New York: Workman Publishing, 1991.

Conde, Délio Marques, et al. "Pseudomamma on the foot: An unusual presentation of supernumerary breast tissue." *Dermatology Online Journal*. 12.4 (2006).

Cheating: Hough, Andrew. "Men more likely to forgive cheating partner's lesbian fling, study finds." *The Telegraph*. 29 Jan. 2011.

"Powerful Women as Likely to Cheat as Men, Study Finds." *Bloomberg Businessweek*. 29 Apr. 2011.

Condoms: "Condoms: Know the Facts." National Health Service. Accessed: 18 Aug. 2010.

Thornton, Jacqui. "The singing protective." *The Sun*. 16 Feb. 2005.

Dating: Campbell, Carolyn. "Speed Dating: A New Form of Matchmaking." Discovery.com. Web. Accessed: 17 Nov. 2011.

Saad, Gad. "Women's Voice Pitch Changes Depending on Their Attraction To a Man." *Psychology Today*. 17 June 2011.

Venezia, Todd. "E-wooed gals say yes to sex." *New York Post*. 24 Jan. 2011.

Exes: Pillsworth, Elizabeth, Martie Haselton and David Buss. "Ovulatory shifts in sexual desire." *The Journal of Sex Research*. 2004.

Honeymoon: "Honeymoon." *World Wide Words*. Web. Accessed: 4 Nov. 2011.

Hormones: Miller, Saul and Jon Maner. "Scent of a Woman: Men's Testosterone Responses to Olfactory Ovulation Cues." *Psychological Science*. 22 Dec. 2009.

Freeman, David. "Women's Tears Turn Men Off: Testosterone Study Explains Why." *CBS News*. 7 Jan. 2011.

Kissing: Kirshenbaum, Sheril. *The Science of Kissing: What Our Lips Are Telling Us*. New York: Grand Central Publishing, 2011.

Cahalan, Susannah. "Birds don't do it, bees don't do it—why do we kiss?" *New York Post*. 2 Jan. 2011.

Love: Nuzzo, Regina. "Rose-colored glasses may help love last." *Los Angeles Times*. 25 July 2011.

Mendick, Robert. "Brain scans reveal power of art." *The Telegraph*. 8 May 2011.

Masturbation: Reber, Arthur S. Rhiannon Allen, and Emily S. Reber. "Masturbation." *The Penguin Dictionary of Psychology*. Web. Accessed: 11 Dec. 2011.

Maines, Rachel. *The Technology of Orgasm: "Hysteria," the Vibrator, and Women's Sexual Satisfaction*. Baltimore: Johns Hopkins University Press, 1999.

Orgasm: Le Page, Michael. "Orgasms: A real 'turn-off' for women." *New Scientist*. 20 June 2005.

Nuzzo, Regina. "Call him doctor 'Orgasmatron.'" *Los Angeles Times*. 11 Feb. 2008.

"Ask Men Great Male/Female Survey 2011." *AskMen.com*. Web. Accessed: 13 Aug. 2011.

Penises: Maugh, Thomas H. "Judging penis size by comparing index, ring fingers." *Los Angeles Times*. 4 July 2011.

Western, Kyle. "Eat This Erection-Boosting Food." *MensHealth.com*. 6 Mar. 2011.

Downs, Martin. "Things You Didn't Know About Your Penis." *CBS News*. Web. 19 Mar. 2008.

Relationships: Bower, Bruce. "Love Makes You Increasingly Ignorant of Your Partner." *Wired.* 14 Oct. 2010.

Semen: Adams, Stephen. "Cooked breakfast 'cuts fertility.'" *Telegraph.* 28 Oct. 2010.

"Men, do you suffer from flu symptoms after sex? You could be allergic to your own semen." *Daily Mail.* 19 Jan. 2011.

Sex Life: Pappas, Stephanie. "Like to Sleep Around? Blame Your Genes." *Live Science.* 1 Dec. 2010.

Hyde, Zoe, et al. "Prevalence of sexual activity and associated factors in men aged 75 to 95 years: a cohort study." *Annals of Internal Medicine.* 7 Dec. 2010.

Freeman, David. "Oral sex now main cause of oral cancer: Who faces biggest risk?" *CBS News.* 23 Feb. 2011.

Singles: Spindel, Janis. *How to Date Men: Dating Secrets from America's Top Matchmaker.* New York: Penguin Group, 2007.

"Singles in the United States." U.S. Bureau of the Census. 2000.

Vaginas: *The Oxford American College Dictionary.* Web. 27 Jan. 2009.

Cheng, "Should You Vajazzle Your Vajayjay?" Shine from Yahoo. Web. 26 Feb. 2010.

Geddes, Linda."Ecstacy over G spot therapy." *New Scientist.* 17 Dec. 2008.

Valentine's Day: "Just in time for Valentine's Day: The heart-shaped island spotted on Google Earth that's become a hit with lovers." Daily Mail. 11 Feb. 2009.

Wiseman, Richard. 59 Seconds: Change Your Life in Under a Minute. New York: Anchor Books, 2009

CHAPTER 3—FRIENDS & FAMILY

Babies: Gooze, Rachel A., Sarah E. Anderson, and Robert C. Whitaker. "Prolonged Bottle Use and Obesity at 5.5 Years of Age in US Children." *The Journal of Pediatrics.* 5 May 2011.

Barbosa, Clarita, et al. "The relationship of bottle feeding and other sucking behavior with speech disorder in Patagonian preschoolers." *BMC Pediatrics.* Sept. 2009.

O'Connor, Anahad. "The Claim: Babies blink less than adults." *The New York Times.* 9 Dec. 2008.

Narvaez, Darcia. "Blame the baby or blame the experts?" *Psychology Today.* 21 Feb. 2011.

Joyner, Brandi, et al. "Infant Sleep Environments Depicted in Magazines Targeted to Women of Childbearing Age." *Pediatrics*. 1 Sept. 2009.

Birthdays: Kesebir, Selin and Shigehiro Oishi. "A Spontaneous Self-Reference Effect in Memory: Why Some Birthdays Are Harder to Remember Than Others." *Psychological Science*. 20 Sept. 2010.

Children: Tierney, John. "Can a Playground Be Too Safe?" *The New York Times*. 18 July 2011.

Wyckoff, Whitney Blair. "Why Keeping Little Girls Squeaky Clean Could Make Them Sick." *NPR Shots*. Web. 3 Feb. 2011.

Friedman, Howard S., and Leslie R. Martin. *The Longevity Project: Surprising Discoveries for Health and Long Life from the Landmark Eight-Decade Study*. New York: Hudson Street Press, 2011.

Adams, Cecil. "Does giving sweets to kids produce a 'sugar rush'?" *Straight Dope*. Web. 15 Feb. 2008.

Dads: Belluck, Pam. "In Study, Fatherhood Leads to Drop in Testosterone." *The New York Times*. 12 Sept. 2011.

"Father Knows Best When He's Thritysomething." *All Things Considered*. NPR. 18 June 1993.

Nock, Steven L. and Christopher J. Einolf. "The One Hundred Billion Dollar Man: The Annual Public Costs of Father Absence." National Fatherhood Initiative. June 2008.

Family Meals: "Children who have family meals are 'less likely to be overweight and binge on junk food." *Daily Mail*. 5 May 2011.

Stein, Jeannine. "Talking with family at mealtime may mean better health for kids with asthma." *Los Angeles Times*. 5 Feb. 2011.

"Sight of Meat Puts People at Ease, Study Suggests." *Bloomberg Businessweek*. 12 Nov. 2010.

Family Size: Saad, Lydia. "Americans' Preference for Smaller Families Edges Higher." Gallup. 30 June 2011.

Friends: Mollenhorst, Gerald, et al. "Social contexts and personal relationships: The effect of meeting opportunities on similarity for relationships of different strength." *Social Networks*. Jan. 2008.

Brashears, Matthew. "Small networks and high isolation? A reexamination of American discussion networks." *Social Networks*. 28 Oct. 2011.

Ridley, Matt. "How Many Friends Can Your Brain Hold?" *The Wall Street Journal.* 12 Feb. 2011.

Grandparents: "Grandparents Day 2006: Sept. 10." U.S. Census Bureau. Web. 10 July 2006.

Phend, Crystal. "Grandparent Driving Means Safer Road Trip." *ABC News.* 18 July 2011.

O'Connor, Anahad. "The Claim: Older People Are the Worst Drivers." *The New York Times.* 20 Sept. 2005.

Specter, Michael. "The Baby Bust: Population Implosion Worries a Graying Europe." *The New York Times.* 10 July 1998.

Households: "Current Population Survey, 2008 Annual Social and Economic Supplement." U.S. Census Bureau. Jan. 2009.

"The Return of the Multi-Generational Family Household." Pew Research Center's Social & Demographic Trends Project. 18 Mar. 2010.

Marriage: "Women gain weight after wedding, men after divorce, study says." *New York Post.* 22 Aug. 2011.

Harrar, Sari and Rita DeMaria. *The 7 Stages of Marriage: Laughter, Intimacy, and Passion.* Pleasantville, NY: Reader's Digest Books, 2007.

Roelfs, David J., et al. "The Rising Relative Risk of Mortality for Singles: Meta-Analysis and Meta-Regression." *American Journal of Epidemiology.* Web. 29 June 2011.

Paul, Pamela. "The Marrying Kind: Born or Made?" *The New York Times.* 14 Jan. 2011.

U.S. Bureau of the Census. 2010.

Moms: Bernhard, Virginia. "Mother's Day." *The Family in America: An Encyclopedia, Volume 1.* Ed. Joseph Hawes and Elizabeth Shores. Santa Barbara, CA: ABC-CLIO Inc., 2001.

"Mother's Day: May 8, 2011." U.S. Census Bureau. Web. 17 Mar. 2011.

Offspring: Newport, Frank. "Americans Prefer Boys to Girls, Just as They Did in 1941." Gallup, 23 June 2011.

Parents: "Speak or Spank? More Parents Choose Reasoning Than Physical Discipline." *C.S. Mott Children's Hospital National Poll on Children's Health.* 16 Apr. 2010.

"Parents Say, 'Other Teens Drink and Use Marijuana—But My Kids Don't.'" *C.S. Mott Children's Hospital National Poll on Children's Health.* 12 Sept. 2011.

Cole, Adam. "Parents' Ums and Uhs Can Help Toddlers Learn Language." *NPR Shots*. Web. 14 Apr. 2011.

Teens: "The Ethics of American Youth: 2010." Josephson Institute Center for Youth Ethics. 10 Feb. 2011

DiSalvo, David. "How We Know You're Lying." *Psychology Today*. 5 June 2011.

Lindenmeyer, Kriste. "Adolescence." *The Family in America: An Encyclopedia, Volume 1*. Ed. Joseph Hawes and Elizabeth Shores. Santa Barbara, CA: ABC-CLIO Inc., 2001.

Toddlers: Alleyne, Richard. "Future criminals could be identified as toddlers." *The Telegraph*. 20 Sept. 2011.

Twins: "Popular names for twins born in 2010." Social Security Administration. Web. Accessed: 18 Nov. 2011.

"Mother's Day: May 8, 2011." U.S. Census Bureau. Web. 17 Mar. 2011.

CHAPTER 4—MIND

Addiction: Brody, Jane. "When Tanning Turns Into an Addiction." *The New York Times*. 21 June 2010.

Colenso, Maria. "10 Strange Addictions." *Discovery Health*. Web. Accessed: 18 Nov. 2011.

Roan, Shari. "Quitting smoking may require longer use of smoking cessation treatments." *Los Angeles Times*. 2 Sept. 2010.

"Crushing Cigarettes In A Virtual Reality Environment Reduces Tobacco Addiction." *ScienceDaily*. 28 Oct. 2009.

Huget, Jennifer LaRue. "Could quitting smoking be a symptom of lung cancer?" *The Washington Post*. 3 Mar. 2011.

Anger: Hughes, Paul M. "Anger." *Encyclopedia of Ethics, Vol I, Second Edition*. Ed. Lawrence Becker and Charlotte Becker. New York, NY: Routledge Press, 2001.

Spiegel, Alix. "Does Getting Angry Make You Angrier?" *NPR*. 26 Mar. 2009.

Daydreaming: Killingworth, Matthew and Daniel Gilbert. "A Wandering Mind Is an Unhappy Mind." *Science*. 12 Nov. 2010.

Decision-Making: Schmid, Randolph. "Facing a Judge? Study Says Go Early or After Lunch." *Associated Press*. 11 Apr. 2011.

Dreams: Alleyne, Richard. "Black and white TV generation have monochrome dreams." *The Telegraph*. 17 Oct. 2008.

Hajek, P. and M Belcher. "Dream of absent-minded transgression: an empirical study of a cognitive withdrawal symptom." *Journal of Abnormal Psychology*. Nov. 1991.

Kinsey, Alfred C., Wardell B. Pomeroy, Clyde E. Martin. *Sexual Behavior in the Human Male*. Bloomington, IN: Indiana University Press, 1998 edition.

Emotions: Parker-Pope, Tara. "Faking Happiness May Lead to Blues." *The New York Times*. Web. 21 Feb. 2011.

Carpenter, Siri. "A Botox gap in understanding emotions." *Los Angeles Times*. 31 May 2010.

Fear: Pizzorusso, Tommaso. "Erasing Fear Memories." *Science*. 4 Sept. 2009.

Parrish, Geov. "Fear of Youth." *Seattle Weekly*. 24 Feb. 1999.

Happiness: Gallup World Poll, 2010.

Gopal, Prashant. "Recession Takes Its Emotional Toll on Cities." *Bloomberg Businessweek*. 26 Feb. 2009.

"America's Happiest Cities." *CNBC*. Web. 22 Feb. 2010.

Tierney, John. "A New Gauge to See What's Beyond Happiness." *The New York Times*. 16 May 2011.

Intelligence: Ayan, Steve. "Smart Jocks: When kids exercise, they boost brainpower as well as brawn." *Scientific American Mind*. Sept./Oct. 2010.

Memory: Feinstein, Justin, Melissa Duff and Daniel Tranel. "Sustained experience of emotion after loss of memory in patients with amnesia." *Proceedings of the National Academy of Sciences*. 12 Apr. 2010.

Williams, Lucy. "Alcohol Boosts Memory, Fights Alzheimer's." *Ivanhoe Newswire*. 27 Oct. 2006.

Alleyne, Richard. "Moderate drinking in old protects against dementia." *The Telegraph*. 22 May 2011.

Lindner, Isabel, et al. "Observation Inflation: Your Actions Become Mine." *Psychological Science*. Aug. 2010.

Migraines: "Precision-Tinted Lenses Offer Real Migraine Relief, Reveals New Study." *ScienceDaily*. 6 June 2011.

Singer-Vine, Jeremy. "For Women With Migraines There May Be a Silver Lining." *The Wall Street Journal*. 15 July 2009.

Positive Thinking: "Positive thinking's negative results." *The Economist*. 13 June 2009.

"Optimism Experts Handicap the Presidential Election." *Penn News*. 26 Sept. 2008.

Post-Traumatic Stress: Vastag, Brian. "Can the Peace Drug Help Clean Up the War Mess?" *Scientific American*. 20 Apr. 2010.

Procrastination: Burka, Jane. *Procrastination: Why We Do It, What to Do About it Now*. 2nd Edition. Cambridge, MA: Da Capo Lifelong Books, 2008.

Fiore, Neil. *The Now Habit*. New York, NY: Tarcher, 2007.

Rationality: Kendrick, Douglas. "How a Passing Mood Can Profoundly Alter Your Economic Decisions." *Psychology Today*. 21 Oct. 2011.

Hsu, M., et al. "Neural systems responding to degrees of uncertainty in human decision-making." *Science*. 9 Dec. 2005.

Lehrer, Jonah. *How We Decide*. New York, NY: Houghton Mifflin Co., 2009.

Reason: Cohen, Patricia. "Reason Seen More as Weapon Than Path to Truth." *The New York Times*. 14 June 2011.

Speech: Greenhalgh, Jane. "A Curious Case of Foreign Accent Syndrome." *NPR Shots*. Web. 1 June 2011.

O'Connor, Anahad. "The Claim: Whispering Can Be Hazardous to Your Voice." *The New York Times Well* blog. Web. 7 Feb. 2011.

O'Connor, Anahad. "The Claim: Humming Can Ease Sinus Problems." *The New York Times Well* blog, Web. 20 Dec. 2010.

Willpower: Hutson, Matthew. "Clenching Your Fists Increases Willpower." *Psychology Today Psyched!* blog. Web. 10 Apr. 2011.

Hutson, Matthew. "Having to Pee Increases Willpower." *Psychology Today Psyched!* blog. 10 Apr. 2011.

CHAPTER 5—BODY

Belly Buttons: Aldhous, Peter. "Scientists find a rich array of unknown bacteria in human navels." *The Washington Post*. 4 July 2011.

Blood: "56 Facts About Blood." America's Blood Centers. Web. Accessed: 15 Nov. 2011.

Pollack, Andrew. "A Blood Test Offers Clues to Longevity," The New York Times, 18 May 2011.

Bones: Carlos Williams, "Ban on bone marrow sales challenged." *Los Angeles Times*. 20 Feb. 2011.

Booty: Macrae, Fiona. "Does my bum look big in this? It better be . . . because it's good for your health." *The Daily Mail*. 12 Jan. 2010.

Brain: Lee Hotz, Robert. "Brain Shrinkage: It's Only Human." *The Wall Street Journal*. 26 July 2011.

Hulihan, Joseph. "Editorial: Ice cream headache." *British Medical Journal*. 10 May 1997.

Timmer, John. "World's total CPU power: one human brain." *ars technica*. 11 Feb. 2011.

Breathing: O'Connor, Anahad. "The Claim: If You're Hyperventilating, Breathe Into a Paper Bag.'" *The New York Times*. 13 May 2008.

Death: "Deaths by State." U.S. Census Bureau. 2010.

Miller, Bill. "Cremation ignites global-warming, atmospheric conflagration." *Desmogblog*. Web. 27 Feb. 2008.

Bowdler, Neil. "New body 'liquefaction' unit unveiled in Florida funeral home." *BBC News*. 30 Aug. 2011.

Disease: O'Connor, Anahad. "The Claim: A person can contract two colds at one time," *The New York Times Well* blog. Web. 17 Nov. 2009.

Singer-Vine, Jeremy. "Blueberries Slow Tumor Growth." *The Wall Street Journal*. 20 Apr. 2010.

Ears: Palmer, Jason. "Background noise affects taste of foods, research shows." *BBC News*. 14 Oct. 2010.

Walsh, Nancy. "Hearing Loss in Teens Linked to Secondhand Smoke." *ABC News*. 19 July 2011.

Espenshade, Linda. "Ear candling." *Intelligencer Journal Lancaster*. 20 Feb. 2006.

Eyes: McCarthy, Claire. "Tear-Free Babies." *Parenting*. 1 Oct. 2007.

Fingers: O'Connor, Anahad. "The Claim: Fingers Wrinkle Because of Water Absorption." *The New York Times Well* blog. Web. 12 Sept. 2011.

Peters, Ryan, et al. "Diminutive Digits Discern Delicate Details: Fingertip Size and the Sex Difference in Tactile Spatial Acuity." *The Journal of Neuroscience*. 16 Dec. 2009.

O'Connor, Anahad. "The Claim: Salons' UV Nail Lights Can Cause Skin Cancer." *The New York Times Well* blog. Web. 2 August 2010.

Hair: "Male Pattern Balding May Be Due to Stem Cell Inactivation." *ScienceDaily*. 6 Jan. 2011.

Wolchover, Natalie. "Scientists Uncover More Secrets of Why Hair Turns Gray." *Life's Little Mysteries*. Web. 16 June 2011.

Wilson, Anthony. "Bald Men More Likely to Develop Heart Disease." *Heart Disease* blog. Web. 3 Feb. 2008.

Heart: Blue, Laura. "When Are You Most Likely to Have a Heart Attack?" *Time*. 22 July 2008.

"Top 10 Amazing Facts About Your Heart." *LiveScience*. 8 Feb. 2007.

Martin, Daniel. "Music to your heart: Listening to John Denver classics can improve your blood flow." *The Daily Mail*. 12 Nov. 2008.

Immune System: "Man flu DOES exist: Women's immune system is much better at fighting off the common cold." *The Daily Mail*. 24 June 2011.

Intestines: Keim, Brandon. "Gut-Bacteria Mapping Finds Three Global Varieties." *Wired*. 20 Apr. 2011.

Itch: Green, Amanda, et al. "Influence of genotype, dose and sex on pruritogen-induced scratching behavior in the mouse." *Pain*. Mar. 2006.

Medicine: Cumbler, Ethan, et al. "Lack of patient knowledge regarding hospital medications." *Journal of Hospital Medicine*. Feb. 2010.

"Sugar Helps Antibiotics Kill Dug-In Bacteria." *Discover*. 16 May 2011.

Sneezes: Roberts, Alan. "Sneeze, if you please: we're not blowing hot air: holding in a sneeze can be harmful." New York, NY: Scholastic Choices, 2006.

Langer, Nicolas, et al. "When the Sun Prickles Your Nose: An EEG Study Identifying Neural Bases of Photic Sneezing." *PLoS ONE*. Feb. 2010.

Sweat: "Women Sweat Less Readily Than Men." *HealthyDay News*. 8 Oct. 2010.

Teeth: O'Connor, Anahad. "The Claim: More Sugar Leads to More Cavities." *The New York Times Well* blog. Web. 16 Aug. 2010.

Tongue: O'Connor, Anahad. "The Claim: Tongue Is Mapped Into Four Areas of Taste." *The New York Times Well* blog. Web. 10 Nov. 2008.

Weight: Szalavitz, Maia. "Marijuana Slims? Why Pot Smokers Are Less Obese." *Time Healthland* blog. Web. 8 Sept. 2011.

Swain, Mike. "'Skinny gene' which makes people thin identified by scientists." *Daily Mirror*. 1 Sept. 2011.

MacMillan, Amanda. "Dieters in Weight Watchers study drop up to 15 pounds in a year." *CNN Health*. Web. 7 Sept. 2011.

Wrists: Park, Alice. "Can Wrist Size Help Predict Children's Heart Disease Risk?" *Time Healthland* blog. Web. 11 Apr. 2011.

CHAPTER 6—WORK

Bosses: McGregor, Jena. "How sarcasm can boost creativity." *The Washington Post On Leadership* blog. 1 Aug. 2011.

"America's Worst Bosses 2010." eBossWatch. Web. Accessed: 15 Nov. 2011.

Singer-Vine, Jeremy. "Venting at the Office Helps Hearts." *The Wall Street Journal*. 1 Dec. 2009.

Burke, Cathy. "Secrets of workers' sex-cess." *New York Post*. 12 Oct. 2010.

Breaks: "Afternoon nap 'is good for heart.'" *BBC News*. 13 Feb. 2007.

Rasch, Bjorn, et al. "Pharmacological REM sleep suppression paradoxically improves rather than impairs skill memory." *Nature Neuroscience*. Web. 5 Oct. 2008.

Venezia, Todd. "A lay at the office." *New York Post*. 15 Nov. 2010.

Calendar: Meeus, Jean. *Mathematical Astronomy Morsels IV*. Richmond, VA: Willmann-Bell, Inc., 2007.

Co-Workers: Lehrer, Jonah, "Are Your Co-Workers Killing You?" *Wired*. 8 Aug. 2011.

Silverman, Rachel Emma. "Hey, You! Mean People Earn More, Study Finds." *The Wall Street Journal*. 15 Aug. 2011.

Desks: Schlosser, Julie. "Cubicles: The great mistake." *Fortune*. 22 Mar. 2006.

Dirty Jobs: Worth, Tammy. "10 Careers With High Rates of Depression." *Health*. 9 Dec. 2010.

Distractions: Silverman, Rachel Emma. "Web Surfing Helps at Work, Study Says." *The Wall Street Journal*. 22 Aug. 2011.

Spira, Jonathan, et al. "The Cost of Not Paying Attention: How Interruptions Impact Knowledge Worker Productivity." *basex*. Sept. 2005.

Langston, Jennifer. "Whining is the worst sound in the world, study confirms." *MSNBC*. 20 June 2011.

Emberson, LL., et al. "Overheard Cell-Phone Conversations: When Less Speech is More Distracting." *Psychological Science*. 3 Sept. 2010.

Drugs at Work: "National Survey on Drug Use and Health." Substance Abuse and Mental Health Services Administration. 23 Aug. 2007.

Feedback: DiSalvo, David. "Expecting Rapid Feedback Makes You Brace for the Worst, While Performing Your Best." *Psychology Today*. 17 Nov. 2010.

Green, Duncan. "Stubbornness Increases the More People Tell You You're Wrong." *Wired Science* blog. Web. 20 Sept. 2011.

Fun: Choi, Charles. "Study's Punch Line: Humor at the Office is Serious Business." *LiveScience*. 7 Nov. 2007.

Interviews: Parker-Pope, Tara. "Beauty Discrimination During a Job Search." *The New York Times' Well* blog. Web. 30 Nov. 2010.

Office Space: Sturcke, James. "Working outdoors reduces male kidney cancer risk, study says." *The Guardian*. 8 Mar. 2010.

Retirement: Westerlund, Hugo, et al. "Effects of retirement on major chronic conditions and fatigue." *British Medical Journal*. 23 Nov. 2010.

Pisarkski, Alan. "Commuting in America III." Transportation Research Board. 16 Oct. 2006.

Safety: "2010 Census of Fatal Occupational Injuries (preliminary data)." U.S. Bureau of Labor Statistics.

Sitting: Lukits, Ann. "Schooling Kids to Wash Hands Cuts Sick Days." *The Wall Street Journal*. 23 Aug. 2011.

Healy, Genevieve, et al. "Sedentary time and cardio-metabolic biomarkers in US adults." *European Heart Journal*. 11 Jan. 2011.

"Ten years in a desk job 'doubles bowel cancer risk.'" *Daily Mail*. 19 Apr. 2011.

Smoking: Lundborg, Petter. "Does smoking increase sick leave? Evidence using register data on Swedish workers." *Tobacco Control*. 2007.

Stock Market: Hansell, Saul. "Bugs and Squirrels Gnaw Away Nasdaq's Image." *The New York Times*. 3 Aug. 1994.

Stress: Park, Madison. "Noisy workplaces could strain heart." *CNN The Chart* blog. Web. 6 Oct. 2010.

Borland, Sophie. "Working an 11-hour day can increase heart attack danger by 67 per cent." *The Daily Mail*. 5 Apr. 2011.

Prehn-Kristensen, Alexander, et al, "Induction of Empathy by the Smell of Anxiety." *PLoS ONE*. June 2009.

Song, Sora. "How hand-washing helps ease your mind." *Time Healthland* blog. Web. 6 May 2010.

Typing: Adams, Cecil. "Was the QWERTY keyboard purposely designed to slow typists?" *The Straight Dope*. 30 Oct. 1981.

Work Schedule: "2009 Vacation Deprivation Survey." Expedia.com. Web. Accessed: 15 Oct. 2011.

Light, Joe. "Leisure Trumps Learning in Time-Use Survey." *The Wall Street Journal*. 23 June 2011.

CHAPTER 7—PLAY

Basketball: Johnson, Kirk. "'Hoosiers' No More, but Heroes All the Same." *The New York Times*. 19 Mar. 1998.

Boating: Nolin, Robert. "Fatter passengers mean fewer on boats." *Sun Sentinel*. 2 Apr. 2011.

Dancing: Choi, Charles. "Study of Men Dancing Reveals Moves Ladies Love." *LiveScience*. 7 Sept. 2010.

Doing Nothing: Eichler, Alex. "Was April 11, 1954 the Most Boring Day in History?" *The Atlantic Wire*. 29 Nov. 2010.

Drinking: "Test-Takers Shrug Off the Effects of Alcohol." *The Wall Street Journal*. 6 Apr. 2010.

"National Survey on Drug Use and Health." Substance Abuse and Mental Health Services Administration. 21 July 2011.

Macrae, Fiona. "Hangovers hit older people harder." *The Daily Mail*. 5 Nov. 2006.

Driving: Watson, Jason, and David Strayer. "Supertaskers: Profiles in extraordinary multitasking ability." *Psychonomic Bulletin & Review*. 2010.

Meditating: Grant, Joshua, and Pierre Rainville."Pain Sensitivity and Analgesic Effects of Mindful States in Zen Meditators." *Psychosomatic Medicine*. Jan. 2009.

Harding, Anne. "In pain? Try meditation." *CNN* Health. 5 Apr. 2011.

Movies: Read, Max. "Researchers Identify Saddest Movie of All Time." *Gawker*. 28 July 2011.

Music: Neighmond, Patti. "How Music May Help Ward Off Hearing Loss As We Age." WBUR. 22 Aug. 2011.

Shute, Nancy. "Take A Deep Breath: That Clarinet Could Be A Germ Factory." *NPR Shots* blog. 31 Mar. 2011.

Outdoors: "2011 Outdoor Recreation Participation Report." Outdoor Industry Association. Web. Accessed: 4 Nov. 2011.

Partying: "World's Strangest New Year Traditions." *Travel + Leisure*. Dec. 2008.

Durfee, Rachel. "The World's Hardest-Partying Generation? 'Cyber Millennials.'" *Popular Science*. 13 May 2009.

Reading: Adelman, James, et al. "Letters in Words Are Read Simultaneously, Not in Left-to-Right Sequence." *Psychological Science*. Oct. 2010.

Kiderra, Inga. "Spoiler Alert: Stories Are Not Spoiled by 'Spoilers.'" UC San Diego News Center. 10 Aug. 2011.

Relaxation: Quittner, Ella. "Hammocks make for deeper sleep." CNN *The Chart* blog. Web. 21 June 2011.

Running: Reynolds, Gretchen. "Nonalcoholic Beer Aids Marathon Recovery." *The New York Times*. 24 Aug. 2011.

Shooting: Mutter, Ryan, and Pamela Owens. "Emergency Department Visits for Injuries Caused by Air and Paintball guns, 2008." Agency for Healthcare Research and Quality. Aug. 2011.

Shopping: Areni, Charles S., and David Kim. "The Influence of Background Music on Shopping Behavior: Classical Versus Top-Forty Music in a Wine Store." *Advances in Consumer Research*. 1993.

"Nielsen Global Online Survey." The Nielsen Company. Dec. 2007. Web. Accessed: 12 Dec. 2011.

Van Riper, Tom. "The World's Largest Malls." *Forbes*. 18 Jan. 2008.

Goudarzi, Sara. "Men as Addicted to Shopping as Women." *Live Science*. 30 Sept. 2006.

Sunbathing: "Chemicals in wine could be used to protect skin from the sun." *The Telegraph*. 31 July 2011.

Rose, David. "Wake up, smell the coffee and go for a run to reduce the risks of skin cancer." *The Times*. 31 July 2007.

Surfing the Web: Locke, Susannah. "New Neurological Evidence That the Internet Makes People Smarter." *Popular Science*. 19 Oct. 2009.

Swimming: "1 in 5 Americans Admit Peeing in Pool." Water Quality and Health Council. 14 May 2009.

Shute, Nancy. "To Avoid Brain-Eating Amoeba, Hold Your Nose." *NPR Shots* blog. 19 Aug. 2011.

Television: "Study: An hour of TV can shorten your life by 22 minutes." *MSNBC.com*. Web. 16 Aug. 2011.

Singer-Vine, Jeremy. "Preschool TV Habits May Hurt Development." *The Wall Street Journal*. 4 May 2010.

Toys: Pisani, Joseph. "The Making of . . . a LEGO." *Businessweek*. 29 Nov. 2006.

Vacation: "2009 Vacation Deprivation Survey." Expedia.com. Web. Accessed: 15 Oct. 2011.

"World Tourism Barometer." UN World Trade Organization. June 2009.

"Blarney Stone named world's most unhygienic attraction." *The Telegraph*. 17 June 2009.

Tugend, Alin. "As vacations shrink, health risk may rise." *International Herald Tribune*. 10 June 2008.

CHAPTER 8—AROUND THE HOUSE

Bathroom: Park, Alice. "Can Overuse of Antibacterial Soap Promote Allergies in Kids?" *Time Healthland* blog. Web. 3 Dec. 2010.

Chores: Davis, Shannon N., Theodore N. Greenstein, and Jennifer P. Gerteisen Marks. "Effects of Union Type on Division of Household Labor." *Journal of Family Issues*. Sept. 2007.

"Modern Marriage: 'I Like Hugs. I Like Kisses. But What I Really Love is Help with the Dishes." Pew Research Center. 18 July 2007.

Lukits, Ann."Many Risks of Shoveling Snow Stressed in New Study." *The Wall Street Journal*. 11 Jan. 2011.

Dogs: Lieber, Alex. "How Do Dogs Sweat." PetPlace.com. Web. Accessed: 1 Feb 2012.

Rice, Sabriya. "Growing body of research says dogs really can smell cancer." *CNN The Chart* blog. Web. 17 Aug. 2011.

Dust: Wewchler, Charles J., et al. "Squalene and Cholesterol in Dust from Danish Homes and Daycare Centers." *Environmental Science & Technology*. Web. 8 Apr. 2011.

Garden: "Gnome expense spared." *BBC News*. 1 Dec. 1997.

"Garden Gnome Liberation Front strikes Paris show." *CNN.com*. Web. 12 Apr. 2000.

Barringer, Felicity. "To Nullify Lead, Add a Bunch of Fish Bones." *The New York Times*. 20 July 2011.

Kitchen: Monwhea Jeng. "Hot water can freeze faster than cold?!?," *American Journal of Physics*. 29 Dec. 2005.

O'Connor, Anahad. "The Claim: Chewing Gum After a Meal Can Prevent Heartburn." *The New York Times*. 31 July 2007.

Pets: "National Pet Obesity Awareness Day Study." Association for Pet Obesity Prevention. Web. 23 Feb. 2011.

"Top 10 Most Popular Pet Names." Petfinder.com. Web. Dec. 2010.

Rabin, Roni Caryn. "In the Home, a Four-Legged Tripwire." *The New York Times*. 27 Mar. 2009.

Sleep: LaRue Huget, Jennifer. "Lack of sleep could lead to weight gain." *The Washington Post*. 2 Aug. 2011.

Alleyne, Richard. "The brain really can be half asleep, claims research." *The Telegraph*. 27 Apr. 2011.

"Elderly Women Sleep Better Than They Think." *ScienceDaily*. 1 Oct. 2009.

Duffy, Jeanne, et al. "Sex difference in the near-24-hour intrinsic period of the human circadian timing system." *Proceedings of the National Academy*. 2 May 2011.

Toothpaste: Devlin, Kate. "Why not brushing your teeth can kill you." *The Telegraph*. 6 Sept. 2010.

Ramirez, Anthony. "All About Toothpaste; Growth is Glacial, but the Market is Big, and So is the Gross." *The New York Times*. 13 May 1990.

"Alcohol drinks flavored toothpastes." Toothpaste World. Web. Accessed: 12 Nov. 2011.

Murano, Gracie. "10 Strangest Toothpastes." *Oddee*. Web. 10 July 2010.

Vacuuming: Bungert, Patricia. *Encyclopedia of Products & Industries—Manufacturing*. Florence, KY: Gale/Cengage Learning, 2007.

Hink, Fred W. and Glen R. Needham. "Vacuuming is lethal to all postembryonic life stages of the cat flea, *Ctenocephalides felis*." *Entomologia Experimentalis et Applicata*. Nov. 2007.

CHAPTER 9—OUT & ABOUT

Air Travel: Nosowitz, Dan. "Fermilab Astrophysicist's Method Cuts Plane Boarding Times in Half." *Popular Science*. 30 Aug. 2011.

Foxwell, Ruth A., et al. "Transmission of Influenza on International Flights, May 2009." *Emerging Infectious Diseases*. July 2011.

"Food-related Clock In The Brain Identified." *ScienceDaily*. 23 May 2008.

Barbecuing: Gardner, Amanda. "Marinades Help Keep Grilled Meat Safe." *The Washington Post*. 22 Aug. 2008.

City Living: Ritter, Malcolm. "Big city got you down? Stress study may show why." *Associated Press*. 22 June 2011.

Plaut, Victoria, et al, "Does attractiveness buy happiness? 'It depends on where you're from.'" *Personal Relationships*. 8 Dec. 2009.

"Grab a towel. Dessert city is America's sweatiest." MSNBC.com. 26 June 2008. Web.

Commuting: "Commuters 'suffer extreme stress.'" *BBC News*. 30 Nov. 2004.

Eisele, Bill, David Schrank, and Tim Lomax. "2011 Congested Corridors Report." Texas Transportation Institute. Nov. 2011.

Pisarkski, Alan. "Commuting in America III." Transportation Research Board. 16 Oct. 2006.

Driving: Carey, Tanith. "SatNav danger revealed: Navigation device blamed for causing 300,000 crashes." *Daily Mirror*. 21 July 2008.

"Scientists Steer Car With the Power of Thought." *ScienceDaily*. 21 Feb. 2011.

Eating Out: Dallas, Mary Elizabeth. "Big fork could be key to small waistline, study says." *USA Today*. 18 July 2011.

Escalators: Schroeder, David. "Why Escalators Bring out the Best in People." *Scientific American*. 29 Mar. 2011.

Symons, Michael. *A History of Cooks and Cooking*. Urbana, IL: University of Illinois Press, 1998.

Exercise: Melnick, Meredith. "Just 15 Minutes of Exercise a Day May Add Years to Your Life." *Time Healthland* blog. Web. 16 Aug. 2011.

Day, Jan. "History of the Treadmill." Livestrong.com. Web. 15 June 2011.

Hu, Winnie. "Double Dutch Gets Status in the Schools." The New York Times. 31 July 2008.

Fresh Air: "CU researchers: Bacteria found in dog poop dominates in air over Cleveland and Detroit." *The Denver Post*. 18 Aug. 2011.

Mobile Phones: Naik, Gautam. "Study Sees No Cellphone-Cancer Ties." Wall Street Journal. 28 July 2011.

Levy, Andrew. "Mobile phones have 18 times more bacteria than toilet handle." *Daily Mail*. 30 June 2010.

Smith, Aaron. "Americans and Their Cell Phones." Pew Internet & American Life Project. 15 Aug. 2011.

People Watching: Bower, Bruce. "Some Fights Vanish In Plain Sight." *ScienceNews*. 16 June 2011.

Public Toilets: Barry, Dave. "Toilet Experiments Can Leave the Uninitiated Quite Flushed." *Los Angeles Daily News*. 30 Apr. 1995.

Greed, Clara. "Public Toilets." *Encyclopedia of Sex and Gender: Culture Society History*. Ed. Fedwa Malti-Douglas. Florence, KY: Gale/Cengage Learning, 2007.

Public Transportation: Troko, Joy, et al. "Is public transport a risk factor for acute respiratory infection?" *BMC Infectious Diseases*. 14 Jan. 2011.

www.mta.info/nyct/facts.

School: Palmer, Kim. "Teens rise but don't shine before school." *USA Today*. 15 Mar. 2011.

Brown, Eryn. "Study links teenage bullying to social status." *Los Angeles Times*. 7 Feb. 2011.

Mueller, Frederick O. and Robert C. Cantu. "Twenty-Fifth Annual Report." National Center for Catastrophic Sport Injury Research. Spring 2007.

Shopping: Dunn, Elizabeth, et al. "If money doesn't make you happy, they you probably aren't spending it right." *Journal of Consumer Psychology*. 21 Mar. 2011.

Dahl, Darren W., Jennifer J. Argo, and Andrea C. Morales. "Social Information in the Retail Environment: The Importance of Consumption Alignment, Referent Identity, and Self-Esteem." *Journal of Consumer Research*. Feb. 2012.

Trains: Ropelk, David. "How Risky is Flying?" *NOVA*. 17 Oct. 2006.

Walking: Wang, Shirley. "Get Out of My Way, You Jerk!" *The Wall Street Journal*. 15 Feb. 2011.

Whyte, John. "Flip Flops: Do They Hurt Your Feet?" *The Huffington Post*. 6 Apr. 2011.

CHAPTER 10—INSECTS

Ants: Binns, Corey. "Why Ants Rule the World." *LiveScience*. 8 May 2006.

Viegas, Jennifer. "Asexual Ants Give Up on Males." *Discover News*. 15 Apr. 2009.

Vastag, Brian. "The incredible floating fire ant." *The Washington Post*. 25 Apr. 2011.

Bees: Wilson, Mark. "Bomb Detector Powered by Bee Tongue." *Gizmodo*. 13 Sept. 2007.

Brahic, Catherine. "Some bees like it hot, others play it cool." *New Scientist*. 19 Jan. 2007.

Marshall, Michael. "Zoologger: The world's smartest insect." *New Scientist*. 17 Aug. 2011.

Dominus, Susan. "The Mystery of the Red Bees of Red Hook." *The New York Times*. 29 Nov. 2010.

Beetles: Wizen, Gil and Avital Gasith. "Predation of amphibians by carabid beetles of the genus *Epomis* found in the central coastal plain of Israel." *ZooKeys*. 20 May 2011.

Dillow, Clay. "Scientists Fit Cyborg Beetles With Generators That Turn Their Own Wings into Power Plants." *Popular Science*. 1 Sept. 2011.

Crickets: Rodriguez-Munoz, Rolando, et al. "Guarding Males Protect Females from Predation in a Wild Insect." *Current Biology*. 6 Oct. 2011.

Sample, Ian. "Largest testicles of any species? That would be the bush cricket." *The Guardian*. 9 Nov. 2010.

Earwigs: Eisner, Thomas, et al. "Chemical defense of an earwig (Doru taeniatum)." *Chemoecology*. June 2000.

Edible Insects: Friel, Sharon, and et al. "Public health benefits of strategies to reduce greenhouse-gas emissions: food and agriculture." *The Lancet*. 12 Dec. 2009.

Flies: "'Paranoia' About Rivals Alters Insect Mating Behavior." *ScienceDaily*. 16 Aug. 2011.

Lice: Corbett Dooren, Jennifer. "Tired of Nit-Picking? Lice Are Peskier Than Ever." *The Wall Street Journal*. 27 July 2010.

Mosquitos: Thompson, Andrea. "How Mosquitoes Walk on Water and Up Walls." *LiveScience*. 18 July 2007.

Shirai, Yoshikazu, et al. "Landing Preference of *Aedes albopictus* on Human Skin Among ABO Blood Groups, Secretors or Nonsecretors, and ABH Antigens." *Journal of Medical Entomology*. July 2004.

Lefevre, Theirry, et al. "Beer Consumption Increases Human Attractiveness to Malaria Mosquitos." *PLoS ONE*. Mar. 2010.

Swarms: Sword, Gregory, et al. "Migratory bands give crickets protection." *Nature*. 17 Feb. 2005.

Simpson, Stephen, et al. "Cannibal crickets on a forced march for protein and salt." *Proceedings of the National Academy*. 15 Mar. 2006.

Snails: Davies, Ella. "Tiny snails survive digestion by birds." *BBC Nature*. 11 July 2011.

Spiders: Agnarsson, Ingi, et al. "Bioprospecting Finds the Toughest Biological Material: Extraordinary Silk from a Giant Riverine Orb Spider." *PLoS ONE*. 16 Sept. 2010.

Venton, Danielle. "Black Widow Spiders Are Wasteful Gluttons." *Wired*. 4 Feb. 2011.

Stings: Backshall, Steve. "Bitten by the Amazon." *The Times*. 6 Jan. 2008.

Schmidt, Justin, et al. "Hemolytic activities of stinging insect venoms." *Archives of Insect Biochemistry and Physiology*. 1984.

Termites: "Incredible Insects." *Encyclopedia Smithsonian*. Department of Systematic Biology, National Museum of Natural History. Web. Accessed: 13 Nov. 2011.

Wasps: Wallace, Amy. "A Swarm of Wasps, if Not Investors." *The New York Times*. 19 Feb. 2011.

Bellows, Alan. "Mind-Controlling Wasps and Zombie Spiders." *Damn Interesting* blog. Web. 7 Sept. 2005.

Worms: Wade, Nicholas. "Roundworm Could Unlock Secrets of the Human Brain." *The New York Times*. 20 June 2011.

CHAPTER 11—ANIMALS

Alligators: Alvarez, Lizette. "In Florida, Gators Are on the Prowl (and in Your Pool)." *The New York Times*. 18 May 2011.

Armadillos: Harris, Gardiner. "Armadillos Can Transmit Leprosy to Humans, Federal Researchers Confirm." *The New York Times*. 27 Apr. 2011.

Bats: Milius, Susan. "Deadly for bugs, perfect for bat naps." *ScienceNews*. 25 Jan. 2011.

Bears: "Melting ice drives polar bear mothers to land." *Reuters*. 12 July 2007.

Warren, Scott. "Need honey? I've got it licked: Meet the bear with the foot-long tongue." *Daily Mail*. 15 Jan. 2010.

Birds: Davies, Ella. "Adaptable urban birds have bigger brains." *BBC Earth News*. Web. 27 Apr. 2011.

O'Luanaigh, Cian. "Zoologger: Bullied boobies develop brain of a bully." *New Scientist*. Web. 28 July 2011.

Chickens: Kram, Yoseph, et al. "Avian Cone Photoreceptors Tile the Retina as Five Independent, Self-Organizing Mosaics." *PLoS ONE*. 1 Feb. 2010.

Chimpanzees: Krief, Sabrina, et al. "Geophagy: soil consumption enhances the bioactivities of plants eaten by chimpanzees." *Die Naturwissenschaften.* 2008.

Crocodiles: Knightley, Phillip. "Simply awesome, nature's perfect killing machine." *The Daily Mail.* 24 Dec. 2003.

Deer: Copeland, Larry. "Teen's death a reminder of deer's threat to motorists." *USA Today.* 30 Nov. 2010.

Dolphins: Langlois, Maureen. "Shark Bites No Match For Dolphins' Powers of Healing." *NPR Shots* blog. Web. 25 July 2011.

Elephants; Bates, Lucy, et al. "Elephants Classify Human Ethnic Groups by Odor and Garment Color." *Current Biology.* 20 Nov. 2007.

Flamingos: Holliday, Casey, et al, "Cephalic Vascular Anatomy in Flamingos (Phoenicopterus ruber) Based on Novel Vascular Injection and Computed Tomographic Imaging Analyses." *The Anatomical Record.* Oct. 2006.

Hares: Holley, Anthon, and Paul Greenwood. "The myth of the mad March hare." *Nature.* 7 June 1984.

Jellyfish: Piraino, Stefano, et al. "Reversing the Life Cycle: Medusae Transforming into Polyps and Cell Transdifferentiation in *Turritopsis nutricula* (Cnidaria, Hydrozoa)." *Biological Bulletin.* June 1996.

Lions: "Top 10 Strange Lion Facts." *Animal Planet.* Web. Accessed: 12 Dec. 2011.

Mice: "Baby mice produced from 2 males." *CBC News.* Web. 9 Dec. 2010.

Monkeys: Gorman, James. "Baboon Study Shows Benefits for Nice Guys, Who Finish 2nd." *The New York Times.* 14 July 2011.

"Bonobo beats chimpanzee in intelligence test." *The Guardian.* 10 Aug. 2011.

Ostrich: Ramakrishnan, Rohan. "The 6 Most Frequently Quoted Bullshit Animal Facts." *Cracked.* Web. 2 Sept. 2009.

Parrots: Coghlan, Andy. "Parrots join apes and Aristotle in the club of reason." *New Scientist.* 22 June 2011.

Pigs: Wang, Ruojun. "China: Pork Powerhouse of the World." 2006 Banff Pork Seminar presentation.

Rats: "US scientists test on-off memory switch in rats." *AFP.* 17 June 2011.

Ravven, Wallace. "Parasite Hijacks Rats' Arousal Circuitry, Study Finds." *The New York Times.* 17 Aug. 2011.

Squid: Owen, James. "Bizarre Squid Sex Techniques Revealed." *National Geographic.* 22 Dec. 2008.

Geere, Duncan. "Giant Squid Could Become Ocean's Panda Bear." *Wired UK.* Web. 9 June 2011.

Suicide: Wobeser, Gary, et al. "Mortality of Geese as a Result of Collision with the Ground." *Journal of Wildlife Disease.* 1 Apr. 2005.

Uribarri, Jaime. "More than 50 sheep commit mass suicide by jumping off cliff in Turkey." *New York Daily News.* 12 Nov. 2010.

Whales: "Killer Whales and the Mystery of Human Menopause." *ScienceDaily.* 1 July 2010.

CHAPTER 12—NATURE

Air: Norton, Amy. "Air pollution tied to babies' ear infection risk." *Reuters.* 2 Dec. 2010.

Clouds: Lloyd, John, and John Mitchinson. "QI: Quite Interesting facts about clouds." *The Telegraph.* 20 Apr. 2009.

Diamonds: Reardon, Sara. "Nanodiamonds Could Be a Cancer Patient's Best Friend." *Science.* 9 Mar. 2011.

Crow, James Mitchell. "Diamond disappears in sunlight." *Nature.* 15 July 2011.

Earth: Plait, Phil. "Ten things you don't know about the Earth." *Discover Magazine's Bad Astronomy* blog. Web. 8 Sept. 2008.

Cain, Fraser. "Interesting Facts About Earth." *Universe Today.* Web. 19 May 2008.

Flowers: McFrederick, Quinn, et al. "Air pollution modifies floral scent trails." *Atmospheric Environment.* Mar. 2008.

Mustain, Andres. "Blooming Corpse Flower Causes Stink, Draws Crowds." *LiveScience.* 10 June 2011.

Fungi: Boyle, Rebecca. "Largest Fungus in the World Found Under Tree in China." *Popular Science.* Web. 1 Aug. 2011.

Gold: Kiger, Patrick J. "10 Surprising Facts About Gold." *Discovery.com.* Web. Accessed: 15 Nov. 2011.

Lakes: Patenaude, Ed. "Indian tale of lake name is one fishy story." *Telegram.* 28 July 2011.

Pappas, Stephanie. "End Times? Texas Lake Turns Blood Red." *LiveScience*. 1 Aug. 2011.

Moon: Chang, Kenneth. "Over a Billion Years, Scientists Find, the Moon Went Through a Shrinking Phase." *The New York Times*. 19 Aug. 2010.

Mountains: Egholm, David, et al. "Glacial effects limiting mountain height." *Nature*. 13 Aug. 2009.

Plait, Phil. "Ten things you don't know about the Earth." *Discover Magazine*'s *Bad Astronomy* blog. Web. 8 Sept. 2008.

Oceans: "Rip Currents: The Ocean's Deadliest Trick." *LiveScience*. 12 July 2005.

Strickland, Eliza. "A Crack Opens in the Ethiopian Landscape, Preparing the Way for a New Sea." *Discover Magazine*. 4 Nov. 2009.

Planets: Solon, Olivia. "Neptune Finishes First Year Since Discovery." *Wired*. 12 July 2011.

"Venetia Phair dies at 90; as a girl, she named Pluto." *Associated Press*. 11 May 2009.

Plants: Karl, Thomas, et al. "Chemical sensing of plant stress at the ecosystem scale." *Biogeosciences*. 8 Sept. 2008.

"Bugs Use Plants as Telephones." *Live Science*. 22 Apr. 2008.

Space: Boyle, Rebecca. "Hazards of Space Would Make Sex Up There Tricky, Say NASA Researchers." *Popular Science*. 14 Feb. 2011.

Schiffman, Lizzie. "FYI: What Does Space Smell Like?" *Popular Science*. 8 Feb. 2011.

Stars: Van Dokkum, Pieter G., and Charlie Conroy. "A substantial population of low-mass stars in luminous elliptical galaxies." *Nature*. Web. 1 Dec. 2010.

Sun: Shipman, James, et al. *An Introduction to Physical Science*. 12th ed. Boston, MA: Houghton Mifflin Company, 2009.

De Pontieu, B. et al. "The origins of hot plasma in the solar corona." *Science*. 7 Jan. 2011.

Temperature: Haines, Malcolm, et al. "Ion Viscous Heating in Magnetohydrodynamically Unstable Z Pinch at Over 2×10^9 Kelvin." *Physical Review Letters*. 24 Feb. 2006.

Trees: Wolchover, Natalie. "How Tall Can Trees Grow?" *Life's Little Mysteries*. 17 June 2011.

"Why Are Tree Rings Lighter or Darker?" *Life's Little Mysteries*. 24 Mar. 2010.

Weeds: Wanjek, Christopher. "The Five Healthiest Backyard Weeds." *LiveScience*. 31 July 2011.

Saccoccio, Sabrina. "Dandelions: Time to throw in the trowel." *CBC News*. 13 June 2007.

THE END

McIver, Tom. *The End of the World: An Annotated Bibliography*. Jefferson, NC: McFarlane & Co., 1999.